These Bright Shadows

The Poetry of Kathleen Raine

⊕

Brian Keeble

These Bright Shadows

The Poetry of Kathleen Raine

⊕

Angelico Press

First published
by Angelico Press, 2020

© Brian Keeble, 2020

For information, address:
Angelico Press
169 Monitor St.
Brooklyn, NY 11222
angelicopress.com

978-1-62138-672-8 pb
978-1-62138-673-5 cloth

Cover lettering by Tom Perkins
Back cover design by Michael Schrauzer

CONTENTS

Preface

WHEN IT CAME TO PUTTING THIS VOLUME TOGETHER, it meant collecting several papers prepared over a period of nearly three decades. There seemed no real prospect of revising the material to make it a seamless whole. It remains, therefore, a collection of separate studies that have undergone some small revision so as to reduce the inevitable overlaps that tend to recur on such occasions. For this reason it is recommended that the reader, rather than work through the collection from start to finish, should consider each study apart from its companions. They are, as it were, a series of regards, each having a focal point that differs from its neighbours that nonetheless is directed towards the same subject—the poet's singular imaginative vision. On each occasion my intention has been to honour the living spirit of comprehension that so evidently is the *raison d'être* of that vision. That intention grew out of my belief that, since, for this poet, poetry is the language of the soul, to present each paper as if it were a contribution to 'English Lit.' (disavowed by the poet) would amount to betrayal of that living comprehension. As the poet pointed out in an essay on David Gascoyne, 'true imagination is an alien presence in any society; always it seems to manifest itself in a way that cannot be explained'.

If there is to be a worthy—if belated—critical assessment of Kathleen Raine's poetry, it must of necessity proceed on the basis of an appropriate understanding: especially in this case seeing that this is a poetry that rests upon premises far removed from the sort of values that, for the most part, are likely to preoccupy both the writer and reader of contemporary poetry. For this reason the reader will find herein very little attempt to 'judge' and every effort to elucidate which it is within my powers to exercise. In his essay 'The Modern Mind' T. S. Eliot observed

> that the poet does many things upon instinct, for which he can give no better account than anybody else. . . . In one sense, but

1

a very limited one, he knows better what his poems 'mean' than anyone else can . . . but what a poem means is as much what it means to others as what it means to the author; and indeed, in the course of time a poet may become merely a reader in respect of his own works.

In her prolific work as a scholar and essayist—laying the 'laborious foundations' as she called it—Kathleen Raine spent little effort elucidating her 'meaning' as a poet; but it becomes evident that these labours give a resonant indication of the premises and values that inform her craft—on which, as a poet, she proceeded and wished finally to be judged. In this respect the interview is especially illuminating and for that reason I have placed it at the head of this collection. As it happens, it forms a perfect introduction in itself to these varied papers now they have been brought together. Reading the interview again after many years I was struck by the depth and clarity with which the poet, in the spontaneity of the interview format, so powerfully implied the 'meaning' of her poetic vision.

My own appreciation of the poetry, which I must confess began slowly, grew as a result of over three decades of friendship. That appreciation did not proceed by any specific discussion with the poet, but rather, as it were, by a process of companionable osmosis. Apart from the interview, the only paper the poet read of this collection was 'Epiphanies of Light', which was written at the poet's request. It remains gratifying to recall that, on reading it, the change of a single word was all the poet called for. All else met with approval.

To my intention in writing these papers I would like to append the hope that, considered together, the reader may find in them a reliably authentic foundation on which to build an appreciation of Kathleen Raine's poetic accomplishment.

Acknowledgements

A small part of the interview appeared in *TR* 2, no. 1 (London, 1979). The whole interview was subsequently printed in *Lindisfarne Letter* 9 (West Stockbridge, MA, 1979). The present text incorporates the poet's many amendments to a copy of this published text and is taken from *Temenos Academy Review* 7 (2004).

'Who Speaks from the Dust?' was originally given as a paper at the Temenos Academy Conference, 'Ancient Springs: the Arts, the Imagination & Our World', St Hilda's College, Oxford, September 2013. It was subsequently published in *The Sewanee Review* (Winter 2016).

'Epiphanies of Light' is reproduced from the author's *Conversing with Paradise* (Golgonooza Press, 2003).

'Poetic Imagination and the Vision of Reality' was the Kathleen Raine Centenary Memorial Lecture of 2008 and was subsequently published as the Temenos Academy's paper no. 28.

'That Dream Is All I Am' is reproduced from *Temenos Academy Review* 14 (2011).

'That Wondrous Pattern' is an adapted and augmented version of the introduction to Kathleen Raine, *That Wondrous Pattern: Essays on Poetry and Poets* (Counterpoint Press, 2017).

'The Making of a Canon' is reproduced from *Temenos Academy Review* 18 (2015).

Not for the first time, it is a pleasure to record my indebtedness to Andrew Frisardi, who has prepared the present text for publication.

An Interview

THE FOLLOWING IS A TRANSCRIPT of a tape-recorded interview with the poet conducted at her Chelsea, London, home on 10 December 1977. It was made at her suggestion and, so far as I know, was the first interview she ever gave, being up to that time rather against the spontaneous format of the recorded interview. Nevertheless, at this stage of her life, she had wanted to make an informal assessment and record of her standpoint and beliefs as a poet. To that end, in a preparatory meeting, we had outlined the direction the conversation should take and I prepared my questions accordingly. I recall being taken aback at the fullness of her responses that so often anticipated and answered the many supplementary questions I had considered.

B. K. *Dr Raine, how did you begin as a poet?*

K. R. My mother wrote down my first poems before I could hold a pencil. I think the reason I became a poet was because I was born into a family to which poetry mattered very much. My father was an English master and taught literature at the local County High School and poetry was my mother's life. She knew great quantities of poetry by heart, Milton in particular and the English Romantic poets. Also she was a Scot and knew by heart a great deal of the Scottish oral tradition, the poetry that had come down to her through that inheritance, so in my childhood I was in an environment of poetry. It was really through my mother that I became a poet; I think there's little doubt of that. And I continued to grow up in a household in which literature was held in high esteem. I had an excellent grounding in poetry and literature through my home, more than through my school. It was simply a household where there were books on the shelves, where my mother very naturally discussed poetry and recited it. It was the air I breathed.

5

How did you learn the craft of poetry? Was this through your parents or at a later stage?

It was really through my parents; and I was at an excellent girls' County High School where we learnt that sort of thing. Schools were more conventional in those days and so we did learn the basic English metres. My father also taught me a good deal about metrics. It so happened that this interested him very much. He was more interested in the structure of language and metrics than perhaps he was in the more romantic side of poetry, which was my mother's concern. He did, in fact, teach me, and I remember it with great pleasure, the classical lyric metres. I didn't learn Latin in school, my father taught it to me. And he taught me a great deal about Latin metrics and the metres of Horace which, of course, are Greek metres. It was a very happy experience to learn these things from my father.

When you speak of your father teaching you, did he teach you as a practising poet himself?

No, my father was a teacher. He could teach anyone anything. He loved literature, but it never occurred to him to practise it himself. He had a very clear and exact mind, and he was deeply interested in the structure of language. He not only knew Latin but Anglo-Saxon very well. I was too idle, I'm afraid, to learn Anglo-Saxon, but he taught me a little of the Anglo-Saxon metrics. These things were what he loved.

You have done some teaching yourself in the formal sense, both at Girton College and at Morley College. In what direction and to what works would you direct a young poet today seriously wanting to learn the craft of verse?

I think simply read the whole of English literature. There is no way of learning about literature except by reading literature. The first steps are always rather unproductive, but as you know, the more you read, so you take more pleasure in seeing the relation, the development of ideas, the channels through which images flow, the changes that come over a literature in the course of time. In fact there is no other way, as Yeats says: 'Nor is there singing school but studying / Monuments of its own magnificence'. You simply must read the literature of your own language, and this I did. When I was educated, we were taught French up to quite a high standard, and I've also read a good deal of French literature with great pleasure, much less of Latin, and a very little Italian. I've simply followed Dante and a few other poets with a translation on the other side. But that is the only way to become a poet: to read poetry, to study poetry, and as you know more so you see more into the development of the language and the way in which it changes and where you yourself pick up the thread. All these things can't be taught. They can only be learned, they can only be discovered in the course of experiencing them for yourself. There are no short cuts. I'm afraid this is an age that wants a quick solution to every problem, and to have some small formula which gives you instant knowledge. But knowledge cannot be had at the cheap rate that this age demands, in any sphere, including that of literature and the arts. The long slow hard way is the only way to achieve excellence in any field. And literature is no exception.

May I suggest that perhaps one might have thought that a poet of your cast of mind would have made more use of traditional forms, whereas in fact very few of your poems are in traditional stanzaic forms. Does this reflect or indicate anything about your attitude towards those forms? I ask this in view of what you said earlier about your father teaching you a great deal about metrics.

When you come to write a poem it's a very different thing from doing an exercise in metrics, because when you are analysing the metrics of older poets you have the poem before you and you dissect what is there. When you are writing a poem the preexisting form does not exist. The form is what comes at the end of the process of writing the poem, not at the beginning. Therefore you are approaching it from the other end. I believe the preexisting forms that we know were spontaneous and came as the natural forms in which certain ideas embodied themselves at certain times for certain poets. The sonnet form, for example, seemed to come so naturally to Renaissance poets, both Italian and English. Now, I know how a sonnet is put together; I could answer an examination paper probably, more or less, on the different forms of sonnets perfectly well. But if I were to write a sonnet this would be a fabrication; a poem would not naturally come to me in sonnet form. The form in which a poem comes is a living form. You have to accept the form that comes to you. Perhaps the sonnet has been written too often. It represents a certain shape of an idea, very beautiful when it comes in that form. Shakespeare's sonnets are so unified and so beautiful. I must say that by the time one gets to Wordsworth the sonnet is already a little tedious, I find. Hopkins perhaps brought it to life again.

Of course I could write a sonnet; I could write any of these forms, but it wouldn't be an imaginative act. It would be a fabrication, an imitation, something which would come from my rational mind and not from my imagination. Forms are born from the Imagination, but they are constructed by the reason. My forms come to me as they must, born from the Imagination. I don't superimpose them by reason; I'm not a poet of that kind. I feel I'm almost apologising for the narrow range of my poems, but in a sense there are certain forms which I use in poetry. There are certain kinds of rhythmic patterns which I can recognise in my poems as being right. I don't use full rhyme very much, but I do attend very much to the rhyme structure of my poems. The recurring or half rhyme in what I write, both at the end of line and also within lines, is very carefully structured if you look at it. Someone else might be able to work it out as a pattern. I couldn't myself because I do it by instinct; but I do it very carefully and I know when it's right. Just lately I have been writing poems of three or four or five lines which are not constructed according to the Japanese haiku pattern but are rather akin to the haiku, in which every syllable is related to every other syllable. They look easy, but they're not. They are very structured forms, in reality, very small structured forms like diatoms or minute organic forms. But, again, in the last few years, I have felt a compulsion to write in this particular form. They are, as it were, given me.

This is what I mean when I say that what we call sapphics and alca- ics and sonnets and villanelles and all these things probably were the forms that presented themselves to the imagination of certain poets at certain times. They were the shape Imagination was taking at certain periods.

The Imagination presents its own forms in a very scrupulous manner. One can be very dishonest in falling into an easy form which rhymes and has a strict metre. One can be carried along with it, one can be carried away with it. Of course, I know that Yeats used the splendid, structured verse he did—traditional metres if you like—but he re-created them for his own purposes and they bear his individual stamp. Every poet, every true poet, leaves his own indi- vidual signature on the verse forms of the language that he uses: Edgar Allen Poe, or Shelley, or whoever it may be. I may have left a small signature in some of my forms; I think that it would be possi- ble for some young literary critic fifty years from now to say, yes, this is a poem by Kathleen. And that is because and in so far as it comes from the Imagination. I'm not foolish enough to think that women are ever going to produce the greatest art in any field. I see myself as a minor poet to whom certain minor forms have pre- sented themselves. You know, the thought of writing a poem on the scale of a Milton or a Dante—one couldn't envisage it. And so the forms that come from my particular imagination are such as you find in my work. When I was younger I was sometimes carried away and added clever allusions, rather defensively. But now I feel confi- dent of my verse forms; I know how to do it. This comes only with practise.

You made a mention earlier of preexisting forms. One thinks immedi- ately of Shelley, how he somehow had a sense of the form before he actually found something to put into the form. Do you think it's more a question of the poet attuning his imagination to this preexisting form rather than a question of going through the mechanics?

Yes, of course it is. Shelley was like a great musician; his verse came to him in great inspired cadences before he had the words to put in it. You can see in his notebooks how these great cadences of verse presented themselves to his imagination, and he couldn't find the words rapidly enough to fill them. I have found this myself in writing poems, that very often what presents itself is a cadence. One can't always find the words that go to the cadence immediately; that takes a little time. But the cadence comes.

Do you find yourself becoming a sort of rhythmic vessel, as it were?

A rhythmic vessel. Yes, like that. That's how they come.

Speaking now as a mature poet, when you're actually working on a poem, have you encountered any impoverishment in current language?

I do find certain difficulties. There are words which, when I was young, I would have used without hesitation because they were current in educated speech. Sometimes I do pause and think, ah, that word may well be obsolete. I do in my writing use a very simple vocabulary, which is probably deceptive because, in fact, the ideas which are often implicit are not simple. But I do very much try to use simple words. Cleverness, you see, is wasted nowadays. When I was young, contemporaries of mine like William Empson, who was a Wykehamist and a scholar at Magdalene College and so on, could air his undergraduate cleverness, and we all enjoyed that very much because that kind of display of erudition was acceptable within that social group. But the ideas were not at all profound. It was simply the style that was erudite and enjoyable in a certain social context. I can't do that, and it seems rather childish to wish to do so, because profound ideas can be communicated in very simple words as we can see from, well, the Gospels, for example. It is a matter of the resonance and depth that one can put into a simple language, not the size of one's vocabulary that counts.

Of course one isn't always sure that people are going to pick up the resonances of one's work, even though the words taken word by word are simple and understandable to anyone. I think this is the central problem. I can't tell what the reader is going to bring to my poems, but as I work on the poem, I try to translate into simple words ideas which perhaps come from a great deal of knowledge of various kinds in many books, which the reader is not going to have read. And how is one going to be sure that the resonance will evoke anything in the reader? There one must simply rely on the fact that in any generation and at any time a human being is still possessed of the levels to which poetry speaks. In a materialist age people still have souls even if they may deny it. One addresses oneself in the poem to the level at which one hopes to be understood, hoping that although a given reader may not have read the same books as oneself, or attained knowledge through the same channels, yet there will be an awareness that receives that which is communicated in the poem. That is the whole art of writing a poem, to make this kind of choice, to try to use valid signs, as David Jones would say; and the question of what are valid signs is a great problem. I think my poems are more accessible than, say, David Jones's because I use nature and cosmology rather than history, because the cosmos is new every day. We awake within the creation. Every morning the sun rises; the world is created, and created at all its levels. If one relied on history, then the signs taken from history that used to be valid are probably no longer valid now for many people. I think David Jones and T. S. Eliot were at a watershed in this respect. On the far side of that watershed we cannot rely on the historic symbols in the same way as Eliot could or David Jones. We have to use, perhaps, cosmological symbols which are unageing, rather than symbols from human history. After all, a great deal of the poetry of the Psalms, the poetry of the Old Testament, is entirely written in terms of the elements of nature, which one can find today just as much as one could then. This is, I suppose, my defence of my own use of nature in my poetry, which is in any case a natural bent of my own, because these are the things I love.

You mentioned in the preface to your Collected Poems (1981) *that you dropped the poems that made use of ecclesiastical symbols, and it is evident in your poetry that you make use of the more immediate symbols of light and water and air. Do you find these are more evocative, more direct in relation to the problem of shared backgrounds?*

Yes. After all, the ecclesiastical symbols, as you call them, which every cultural tradition possesses—certain things used in a special way—in turn are all finally rooted in water, air, light, the growth of a plant, animation, different animal symbols. It all comes back to the immediate language which God speaks to every man every day, in the rising of the sun, the darkness and light; growth, the flowing of water, the crossing of the sea. All these things are the foundations of all symbolic traditions, finally. They take on more specialised meanings at certain cultural periods, certainly. And when I use, for example, wind or light or reflection in my poetry, I am perfectly aware of at least the Neoplatonic or Christian uses of these symbols, but they have to be restated in such a way that the reader can discover them anew. I am aware of how such a symbol comes to us loaded with the experience of generations of human beings who have experienced these things immediately from nature, and who have also experienced them in some metaphysical tradition. But one has to cleanse them and try to re-present them without losing any of the meaning which, say, Plotinus, or whoever it may be, has given to these symbols, and do so without actually mentioning or invoking Plotinus. If you have to put in the name of Plotinus, you are really confessing defeat as a poet, because the poem should communicate without that.

I feel this is a quality you share with, for instance, Vernon Watkins in his use of the symbol of light. It's perfectly possible to read through a poem by Watkins and appreciate the symbol of light which is underneath most of his poetry, and yet at another level one can associate it with Neoplatonic doctrine. I was very interested to read recently in a book on Watkins that he actually kept the Enneads *on his desk. Did you know that?*

Yes, I remember his telling me so. That's something we have in common, because I keep the *Enneads* near also. Watkins is an excellent example of what I mean, because, as you say, it is possible to read him without knowing the *Enneads*, and yet we would agree that he does in his poems embody all that he needs from the *Enneads*, without having to underline the fact that he is drawing on this source.

An Interview

It seems as if he is speaking of the natural world, but there is no doubt that it is a natural world transfigured, not just a material world of corporeal light, as Blake might have said.

Indeed it is. But, you see, according to the depth of our understanding, so the world we perceive reflects that depth. As Blake said, 'A fool does not see the same tree as a wise man sees'. Vernon Watkins was really experiencing the physical world in a totally different way from the materialist, because the light he saw was filled with a spiritual illumination as well as a physical visibility. He was giving in his poems a living experience, his own living experience of real light as he saw it from his little house on the west coast of the Gower Peninsula. When he saw the light on the sea, he experienced that light in terms of the depth of his own knowledge, so there is a meeting of the knowledge and the actual corporeal experience which comes through in the poetry. It isn't that everyone sees the world in exactly the same way, but some people add a little metaphysics from a tradition and others don't do so. The experience itself of seeing is transformed, as we transform ourselves by the depth of our own understanding of the world, which comes to us through many channels—through life and through learning and through reading the great books of all religions.

The question of the poet having his metaphysics in his heart rather than in his head.

Oh, certainly. It is only the metaphysics that the poet has in his heart that is of the slightest use in his poetry. If poets have their metaphysics in their heads only and try to write verse, it doesn't work. It is only living experience that emerges in poetry, and this is just as true of the experience of the intellect as it is of the physical experience. Dante lived his metaphysics. It wasn't something he knew and added to his earthly experience; it was experience of the heart. That is why poetry and the arts are so testing, because you can't get away with falsehood. The poem will only tell the truth that you know with your whole life and being. Anything added is just trimmings. It's nothing at all. You can bespatter your verses with all kinds of learned allusions, but it doesn't in the least communicate the knowledge that the names you may put in are intended to communicate. You can only communicate what you have lived in a work of art.

Do you think that Eliot and Pound were to some degree guilty of this?

I think Eliot and Pound are very different. Pound was a man of letters. He really became excited by literature; it had a magical spell for him, and he managed to communicate this. His love for a certain range of literature communicates itself in his work. I was thinking of poets not nearly as good as Pound, although Pound isn't my favourite poet. But I would give him his due, that his enthusiasm for letters was probably the most authentic thing about him as a poet. I think Eliot used those learned allusions of his in a different way. I feel they were rather the mask, or the camouflage almost, with which a very passionate and tormented soul gave a kind of dignity and objectivity to passions that were perhaps so searing and so intimately personal that he couldn't have endured to expose them more nakedly. He was using a seemly mask by invoking Lancelot Andrewes, and that rather dignified procession of names that we find in his work. When I read *The Waste Land* now I am struck not so much by the learned allusions that need footnotes, which indeed did impress us when we were young, but by the anguish behind that mask of dignity which he had to assume for his own protection.

One gets the impression from so much poetry today that poets are desperately trying to manipulate the limbs of an organism that is essentially dead, or at least it will not yield quite what they want it to, and that leads to some desperate innovations—at its worst, for example, concrete poetry.

I think it yields exactly what they want it to. It's a great fallacy that poetry is somehow going to save the culture to which it belongs. In fact, poetry can only express the culture from which it springs, and this kind of rubbish that one sees so much of, which is, as you say, totally bankrupt, is expressing only too well the bankrupt situation of materialist society. The materialist view of reality is in its very nature incapable of producing great art, because it denies those levels of the human being from which Imagination speaks and of which poetry and music and the other arts are the language. If you deny the soul and the spirit you have cut off the possibility of the very expression of the soul and the spirit, which is art. You cannot have poetry which comes only from the material level of experience. It is simply not possible. You can have on that level, if you like, political verse, you can have wit, you can have to a certain extent, although one sees all too little of it, comic verse. You could even have, in a more elegant age, the mannered verse of the Augustan poets. But if you deny the reality of the human soul and the spirit which informs it, poetry ceases to be possible, because poetry essentially, as I understand it, is the language of the human soul, through which the spirit speaks. It is not the language of the temporal human being in a material world. And if these people were honest, they would say they have no use for poetry and the other arts in their kind of world. The kinds of things you are referring to like concrete poetry are just not poetry although harmless and sometimes amusing. Hamilton Finlay's garden is a pleasant, imaginative spot, but it's of no importance from the point of view of poetry. It is in a sense rather magical; I see him as a sort of poor man's Capability Brown with a sense of fun added, and I've no wish to decry this. But we poets are trying to do something different.

Can you say something about the difference between what you refer to, in speaking of your own work, as a simple style in contrast to a colloquial idiom?

By the colloquial idiom I think you mean the kind of poetry that accepts with the colloquialisms the whole world that they imply. The poet is putting himself on the level of the colloquialisms, rather than raising the level of discourse, as Blake, for example, did in *Songs of Innocence* by giving people simple words upon which they can ascend to the meaning of the poet. The poet comes down to the level of his readers rather than leading the readers, through words that are familiar to them, up to the level of the poetry. Many poets do like to come down to the level of their readers, presumably in order to have readers. I don't know whether it works; it probably doesn't, in the long run.

On what ground must the battle for the future of poetry be fought if it is to survive being buried beneath the accumulated detritus of what we are pleased to call culture these days?

It can't be buried, because humanity doesn't change. Reality is always what it is, and human beings are not in reality different now than in any other age. Fashion can't change the real nature of man; and because man is man we have in ourselves a certain nature which responds to certain themes and experiences. I believe it is always possible for a great poet who speaks from the fullness of his humanity, to find a response in other human beings who share that humanity. The function of the arts is surely to awaken in people self-knowledge, knowledge of the scope and scale of their own humanity, which they may not have been aware of. It is an enlargement of experience. In almost every respect Yeats's view of the kind of world we live in is diametrically opposite to the view of the world which is put about by the mass media. Yet what a response Yeats has awakened by his poetry in many people who couldn't have accepted or understood the ground from which it undoubtedly grew. Now we see that people are even beginning to take his ideas seriously because they have come to realise through his poetry some of the depth from which that poetry itself arose. I think it can always be done. The question is the genius of the poet. If one is good enough one can awaken the response in human beings that one would wish to awake. One awakens by one's work exactly that level in other people to which the work is adequate. Of course, there are a great many people who don't respond, but some do. I would never despair. I don't think that the mere fact that we are in a very low and dark period culturally is any excuse for poets not writing to the height of their powers; in fact you have to be rather better than not so good. You have to aim even higher in order to get your response, not lower, in such an age. It's a great mistake to think that by coming down and writing colloquial idiom you will do this. You won't. You will do it, perhaps, by being as good as Yeats.

Much of your poet's learning has taken place at the confluence of the traditions of both East and West. How do you view the apparent abandonment of all that was meant by a classical education in favour of what appears to be, in the hands of the young, a cursory knowledge of the traditions of the East?

Well, of course I greatly regret the abandonment of such treasures of civilisation as we have in the West, without in the least wishing to discourage anyone from searching in the East or in any other tradition. It is not what the young are learning from the East that I deplore, but what they are not learning from the West. Knowledge is always good and ignorance is always bad. The crossroad situation is one in which I have certainly felt myself very much involved; I have read a certain amount of Eastern philosophy, from which I have received a great deal of enlightenment of my own tradition. In fact, Christianity seems plausible in the light of Indian Buddhist and Vedantic teaching in a way that it never seemed plausible to me as it was presented by the rather unenlightened teachers from whom I received it as a child. I think that every tradition can receive replenishment from other traditions without one's having to abandon one's own. This seems to me to be a good thing. I do regret the failure of our own tradition; that is very regrettable. But I don't regret the curiosity about other traditions, and I find the hippies and the generation who have been making their pilgrimages to the Far East very touching. They may learn at a very superficial level, but at least they are seeking for something. I don't deplore their search. I may deplore their ignorance, but not their search.

I think it was Coomaraswamy who made the point that the only real reason to have a knowledge of another tradition is that that knowledge should plunge one back into the roots of one's own tradition.

Yes, I think this is very important because any religious tradition, Vedanta certainly, and the American Indian too, would say that the time and place into which we are born is no accident. We are born exactly where it is appropriate for us to be, and therefore we must not deny that which we receive by being born where we are. We can't remake ourselves. I have tried very hard, as you know, for a whole lifetime to make a Christian of myself, simply on those grounds. I was born within what one may call Christendom, and must make the best of a bad job, if you like. I have often felt that I very much wished I were born elsewhere and in another time. I would much rather, so I have fancied, have been born in the time and place of Pythagoras or Plotinus, or maybe in India or in Buddhist Japan. But as this has not been the case I have felt it was necessary to come to terms with who one is and where one has been situated. David Jones also felt this was very important. We must use what comes to our hands. Of course, what comes to the hand of anyone born in the modern world, in the second half of the twentieth century, is a situation of the confluence of cultures, and it would be just as artificial to exclude other cultures as it would be to abandon one's own. One cannot any longer be the kind of Christian that it was possible to be in the seventeenth century, for example, who was totally ignorant of other religions. It is very noticeable among my various friends who are interested in the Perennial Philosophy in one way or another, that they all speak of the necessity of adopting one tradition, but many of them have not adopted the tradition to which they were born. This is a situation of mixing cultures which we can't exclude at this time. One can't exclude what comes to one, because there it is; it comes. It's rather difficult to keep one's bearings in this situation, and very important to do so—also very exciting to do so. I find it a very enriching and interesting experience to live at this time.

Of course, knowledge of the classical world has again and again proved itself capable of being a regenerative experience, hasn't it?

Our Western European tradition, by which I mean the Platonic and Neoplatonic metaphysics, has been equal to any other tradition. There is no need to go further afield; it is all there and very splendid and full. It lacks nothing of the completeness of any other tradition of the Perennial Philosophy. When I was young, knowledge of the Greek myths was almost taken for granted; one learned them as a child. There were countless books for children or for young people about Greek mythology; this was in every child's ordinary upbringing. I certainly learnt all these things long before I went to school. I found in teaching at Girton College, Cambridge, that the students did not know the classical myths, and it is a great loss to the younger generation now. But certainly wherever the Neoplatonic tradition has surfaced in Western culture, as at the time of the Renaissance or of the Romantic poets in England, or in Germany, or again in the Irish Renaissance, it has always had a power of fertilizing and regenerating the poetry or the thought of its time. Truth never becomes out of date; it is always itself and is always there for those who wish to avail themselves of it. It can never lose its validity.

If I may come back to your own work for a moment, it could be said that in its entirety your work throws out a challenge to the values of the contemporary literary world.

Certainly my work throws out, if you like, a challenge, but I don't think of it as a challenge to the received values of the world I live in, but rather as an attempt to affirm the enduring values in so far as I have discovered them. This I have tried to do in various ways, as you know: in my Blake scholarship, in such criticisms as I have written, in my work on Thomas Taylor, and in my poetry certainly. This is the ground from which my poetry comes. I'm not concerned with the literary world. I don't see the literary world and the work it produces in prose or verse as something in itself. There is no such thing. The literary world is only expressing the culture in which it is rooted. In so far as what you call the literary world is an expression of current ideologies, that doesn't concern me at all. It is a different order of values from my own work. I am trying to embody certain realisations which, over the course of a lifetime, I have come to value. In a way, you see, I am speaking to the people who belong to a different culture from what you call the literary world, which is only the articulation of the culture for which it speaks. I have nothing in common with another person just because he or she happens to write verse. The people with whom I have something in common are the ones who share my premises and experience of reality. There used to be talk about two cultures, and I very much believe there are two cultures, but the division doesn't come between the literary world and the non-literary world; it comes in a different direction altogether. It comes in a certain view of man. There is the culture of a materialist view of man, which, as I take it, underlies the kind of colloquial verse you were speaking of earlier, and there is the culture of the spiritual view of man. And that for me is where the division comes. I have everything in common with those, whether of the past or of the present, who participate in the spiritual view of man and nothing in common with the others. I know myself to be to a great extent, though not totally, isolated as I stand now. But after all, I have on my side the great poets of the past and many of my contemporaries, whom I have known among my friends: David Gascoyne, Edwin Muir, Vernon Watkins, T. S. Eliot. I didn't actually know Yeats, though I did know Mrs Yeats after his death. One doesn't feel all that isolated, you know, because the spiritual view of man has never been totally destroyed in the world.

When I was young, you see, literacy was rather different. One had something in common with people because there was a certain level of what one might call secular culture, which was a shared common ground between believers and nonbelievers over a certain area. And there is a certain spiritual resonance, for example, in, well Proust obviously. Who could say whether Proust was a believer or nonbeliever; it hardly matters. He had a certain imaginative depth and resonance, as did even Virginia Woolf in certain areas of her experience—there was an overlap. Now, with a totally secular culture, the division is really much more clear-cut. There is really literally nothing in common between the profane culture of this time and the other side which I try to express. The rift is much clearer. It's perhaps regrettable that there no longer is any common ground of the old European secular culture on a very high level, which existed up to the middle of the Second World War, but seems to have disappeared since. I literally find I have nothing in common with secular, or rather, indeed one can only say profane, writers who have no spiritual root in their work. That is a very painful thing, to be in such a situation. It was much happier in the old days when there was this area of common ground, where one could share certain values which belonged to European civilisation, which of course originally had its spiritual roots. And a great deal of this still continued in modes of feeling, manners if you like, modes of behaviour, which though not immediately rooted in a spiritual vision were ultimately rooted in a civilisation which itself had such roots. Such European Christendom has now virtually ceased to exist in this country. It still lingers on in France, where I feel very much more at home than I do in England, culturally speaking, or in Italy, or maybe in Spain. I may be overoptimistic in that, because I think the whole thing is doomed.

You have often observed that in our time ignorance sits in judgement over knowledge. Could you spell out some of the more dangerous varieties of this disease?

The most dangerous variety of the disease is to suppose that man exists only on a horizontal plane, as a biological being in a material world. It is the discounting of what one might call the vertical dimension of our humanity that is most dangerous. You see, materialism tries to reduce all things to the quantifiable. Now, life cannot be quantified, consciousness cannot be quantified; and by saying that only the quantifiable is real, by identifying reality with the materially measurable and materially quantifiable, you are in fact cutting away the greater part of our humanity, which is not quantifiable, which exists in, one can but say, higher dimensions. Life, consciousness, self-consciousness: these are all degrees and modes of experience which cannot be evaluated in material terms. And in so far as materialist philosophy tries to reduce consciousness, for example, to the organ of the brain through which consciousness is registered, it is trying always to reduce the higher experience to some lower term than itself, instead of seeing the lower, quantifiable, material level as itself a reflection which is created by the higher levels of reality. In fact, the most dangerous of all illusions is to suppose that the material world completely accounts for all reality and all human experience. Far the most dangerous.

As an autonomous world, in fact.

As an autonomous world, yes. That is the heresy.

As a writer who has borne witness to a very different set of values to those commonly operative in our society, what has it meant to you to be constantly going against the grain in this way?

Well, I've found it very invigorating in so far as my scholarship is concerned. It's given me something that I felt was important to do. It has seemed to me worthwhile doing this even though I may not be the most qualified person to do it; at least it has meant that what I was doing had a real value. It has been a challenge, and I've very much enjoyed it. I am very happy to have had the opportunity of doing this particular piece of work in my time and place.

Now that the 'culture wallahs', as David Jones might call them, have capitulated so completely to the 'entertainment wallahs', would you go so far as to say that we are living in times that are without culture?

Pretty nearly so.

One often meets with the expressed fear of the breakdown of culture. At what point does culture break down for you?

I think when the allusions are no longer received. You see, in any work of art the subtle allusions that one is constantly making, not necessarily quotations from Shakespeare, but words and ideas, are used on the supposition that the reader is going to share that ground sufficiently to respond to certain symbols. If one said the Cup are they going to think of the Grail, or if one said the Cave are they going to think of Plato? These are rather poor examples, but all the time the poet is working upon a shared background of language and literature and religion and history, which one has to play on like an instrument. One sounds the language like a sounding board on the supposition that within one's own society people will know what one is talking about and respond to those allusions which are the essence of communication. When this is no longer so, then that culture has broken down. I think we've come very near that point now.

An Interview

In your paper on David Jones ('David Jones and the Actually Loved and Known') you mentioned the scholar Edith Hamilton's definition of a barbarian as someone who does not know his or her past.

Yes, who has no past. And against that one could place Eliot's remark, I hope I quote it correctly: 'We know more than the past; yes, and the past is what we know'. Within a civilisation the whole of the past is contemporaneous. We read Homer, and Achilles and that great battle outside Troy becomes for us contemporaneous; it is part of our present. The life of Jesus Christ is contemporaneous. This is the quality of the mind: all things within the regions of the mind exist contemporaneously. All are just as present to us as what we hear on the news this evening. It is a terrible situation when the present of people is so narrow that it only includes what happened to them this week. This is terrible. The whole purpose of human culture and civilisation is to expand the area of the present to include great areas of the past, remote other times, other lives, other civilisations. A truly civilised person is one whose interior experience embraces great areas of what has happened in the past and in other cultures. To be an uncultured person is to have none of this.

A cultured person would indeed be able to relate the historical process itself, however broadly, to that which was above and beyond the historical process as well, do you think?

Well, I was speaking then only of culture, and I would say that culture has broken down when a total body of knowledge which belongs to a civilisation is no longer a shared knowledge. But, of course, beyond that, every great civilisation has itself been rooted in some metaphysical vision or premise from which its culture has flowered, as Christendom flowered from the vision which came into being at the time of Christ. And all its art, its music, its expression has, as it were, been like the foliage borne on that tree. And so with Islam, or with Far Eastern Buddhist civilisation; it always is the flower. Of course, the culture is the flower on some living root of that kind, and that is certainly very important. When it is severed from that root it will not long survive—as we see in the decline of our own secular culture.

Would you say that, for the poet, culture is inherent in the accumulated connotations of words?

Yes, and that was why earlier, when you asked me what the best training for a poet was, I said to read the whole of the literature of that language, because that is the way in which we become familiar with the meanings of words, their connotations, their resonances, which is the instrument upon which any poem must play. And when these allusions, connotations, resonances are lost to a society as a whole, then poetry of real quality becomes impossible, quite apart from the metaphysics of the situation. This is purely on a cultural level. There, I would say, is the breaking-down point of culture of which you asked me just now—when the words no longer are embedded in the total matrix of a language which itself is the total product of a culture reaching back to the very beginnings of language. It is only from the whole of a culture that words derive any meaning whatsoever. There is nothing inherently meaningful in a word. A word is simply a magical sign that in the course of history has gathered about itself certain meanings. Therefore, the only way in which a poet can use words with mastery is to familiarise himself with words in the context in which they have been used. The same applies to verse forms; you will learn better how to use verse forms by familiarising yourself with the works of those poets who have used those forms than by taking an abstract pattern and trying to use it yourself. You can't isolate one part of a language. Self-expression is really a fallacious notion which is much too prevalent, because if we were really, totally left to our own resources and were expressing only ourselves we would have neither the words to express ourselves with, nor a context of culture which would make these words communicable to others.

I believe you destroyed your first attempt to write about Blake.

Yes, I did. I didn't at the time possess the adequate knowledge for a study of Blake. I had seen, as many others have before and since, that the basic psychological pattern which Blake was uncovering was very similar to that described by Jung—the fourfold structure of the psyche and the anima and so on—and my first attempt on Blake was rather a Jungian interpretation. However, at that time, Philip Sherrard lent me several books by René Guénon which completely transformed my view of the whole matter. The idea of a tradition of esoteric knowledge and an accompanying language of symbols was new to me, and I immediately, or very soon, realised that this was the key to Blake, that he was in fact working within a traditional language, using that traditional symbolic language in a strictly objective way, and was not to be understood in terms of a personal system—as many had previously thought—invented by himself. And this indeed proved to be the right key. After that I decided to discover where Blake had made his links with tradition and set myself the task of reading everything that he mentioned having read. By the time I had done so, I had come upon a whole body of what one can only call excluded knowledge upon which he was drawing: knowledge of a spiritual tradition which was based on premises other than the materialist society in which we are and indeed in which Blake was living. It is a very venerable tradition indeed, going back to Plato and the Neoplatonists. He knew a little of the Vedanta, he knew something of Cabbala; fewer texts were available to Blake than are available to us, but at least he drew upon a coherent tradition of knowledge based on the premise that mind or spirit is the ground of reality and not matter. And that was the key.

Was it your work on Blake or your reading of Jung that was instrumental in 'de-solidifying' what must have seemed the exclusively positivist and materialist world of your Cambridge days?

It was both. I was reading Jung before I was reading tradition. Certainly he achieved a great deal of desolidification, but I had no conception of the strength of the traditional position until I had done a very great deal of reading in relation to my work on Blake. And it was like melting an iceberg, but the iceberg had nearly totally disappeared by the time I'd covered all the ground of this beautiful, coherent, and highly organised body of philosophy and knowledge.

Your frequent references to Jungian ideas have about them a certain note of ambivalence. You speak of him as being the one teacher of your generation to whom you are most indebted, yet you also claim you are not a Jungian. Can you explain?

I would never commit myself totally to being a follower of anyone, not even William Blake. In fact, Jung and Blake derived their particular knowledge both from the same sources. Both were deeply versed in Gnostic literature, for example. Jung, I think, had a particular function to perform, which was to reopen in this century the inner worlds which had been virtually lost. Certainly Freud discovered, or rediscovered, the unconscious, but he did not for a moment realise what a great continent he had brought to light. It was Jung who realised this; that the inner worlds are not simply regions of knowledge repressed from consciousness. Freud's philosophy is a materialist philosophy: there is nothing in the unconscious that hasn't come through the world of the senses. Jung realised that the psyche is living and has its own laws, and its own structures, and is to each individual an oracle in the heart which mediates from—he would never quite say, but he never quite unsays it either—a divine source to the human. Jung was very careful to keep his teaching within the terms of medical science, because he knew that if he did not do so he would be dismissed as a crank. From *Memories, Dreams, Reflections* we know that he did wholly believe in God and that the oracle in the heart he did see as the immediate presence of God to every individual.

Now, I couldn't call myself a Jungian because I spent twenty-five years on unravelling Blake's teaching. If I were to call myself an adherent of anyone, it would be Blake rather than Jung, because I think Blake set forth more fully, more perfectly, more convincingly than even Jung did, his system. The other reason why I could not totally call myself a Jungian, is that tradition is not a purely subjective thing, that we cannot live entirely from inner revelation without the support of revealed tradition as this is understood by all the great religions. Such figures as the Buddha or Jesus Christ or Muhammad have a function within a total society to bring a new revelation to a whole group of people. Although we cannot experience these things otherwise than within the psyche, nevertheless a revealed tradition holds before us knowledge which we have to work towards, so I think the collective revelation is also important. We can't live entirely without that side, not entirely from the psyche.

You have written that Jung is less poetic than Plotinus or Proclus.

I can't remember when I said that or what I meant at the time, but what I perhaps meant was that the total cosmology of Plotinus, or the Neoplatonists, is wider in its embrace than the psychology of Jung. The total cosmology of Platonism presumes four worlds, of which the psyche is one. Jung, without denying the existence of the other worlds, is speaking only of the psyche. Where he is of great importance is that it is within the psyche that we as human beings must experience the symbols which Plotinus, as a great mystic, also perhaps experienced on higher levels, levels which Jung leaves with, I think, considerable tact, perhaps because he himself was not concerned with them. But in defence of Jung I must say this: that it is within the psyche that we encounter reality; this is where the symbols come to meet us. We know that a certain symbol is valid when we encounter it in our own dreams or visions. There is no argument, because that is a living experience. From that point of view our debt to Jung in this age is boundless, because there's no question that the symbols of the churches and so on have become purely external and dead, unable to reawaken in believers in a certain religion the living experience from which they originally sprang and which they, in an age of living faith, can mediate. Jung restored the living source. Of course, he didn't, as Plotinus did, relate this to a total cosmology; that wasn't his function. He didn't deny a total cosmology, which I suppose Freud did. He is an open-ended psychologist; this is his great merit. Others like to close their systems, but Jung left his open.

Do you agree that some of the followers of Jung are in danger of blindly seeing the psyche as all?

Some may be and others not. There are a great many followers of Jung who are following their own religious tradition, as indeed Jung very much advised people to do. When he had, as it were, completed a cure, he very often found that the patient would spontaneously return to whatever religious tradition they had originally come from, and Jung regarded that as a very desirable end to achieve. There is nothing in Jungian psychology that is incompatible with the adherence to some religious tradition; on the contrary. On the other hand, no doubt there are Jungian psychologists who do not belong to such a tradition. Jung himself said, on British television, when he was asked whether he believed in God: 'That is a very diffi-cult question because I don't believe, I know'. Knowledge is different from belief, you see. Jung at least made that clear to all who have come under his influence, that to know a thing is a very vital experi-ence, whereas believing can mean nothing at all.

Marco Pallis considered the Neoplatonic learning as being dead. Yet there is something about that learning that poets refuse to let die. Blake and Shelley and Yeats and Vernon Watkins and yourself have all found something living in this body of knowledge.

Yes. This is a very interesting point really, because Marco would not regard Neoplatonism as a valid living tradition in which one could participate, as one can participate in those religions which have, for example, a liturgy. Neoplatonism exists now only, if you like, in books. But as a poet it has for me been the most living tradition of all. I would never deny my Neoplatonism; I am a very knife-edge Christian indeed. The poets certainly have kept the tradition of Neoplatonism alive in Europe, whether within Christendom or out-side it; it is the real religion of the poets. What Marco perhaps felt was lacking in Neoplatonism is something that Christian worship offers, which is a point of meeting between the wise and the igno-rant, common humanity and learning: a point at which you can share the symbols at every level with people of every kind. I think this is important, and it's something that I've felt as a lack, certainly, in my life. This is why I keep trying to go back to the Church, although I'm never very happy when I get there. But it is something that is very important to poets, not to live in a rarefied world where there is no common language or shared symbolism with living people.

What do you understand by tradition?

You're leading me into very deep waters. Tradition is knowledge absolute of the nature of man and his place in the cosmos. Absolute, that is, in relation to our own human potentiality, because one cannot know beyond our humanity. Now this knowledge has been revealed in the several great religions of the world, and indeed to primitive people within their own terms, even in the most simple cultures as, for example, the American Hopi Indians, whom I was fortunate to meet a year ago. It is sometimes called the Perennial Philosophy. It is true in an absolute sense, no less so now than in the past or in the future.

Can you say what you don't mean by tradition?

Certainly I do not mean what Dr Leavis meant by tradition, which was simply anything that may be handed on within a society from one writer to another, say style or subject matter, which could be true or untrue or valuable or less valuable; it would be simply the transmission of anything or everything from generation to generation. And this could include falsehood as well as truth; it could include the tradition that runs from Bacon to Newton and Locke to Darwin and so on. But this is not what is meant by tradition among those who have familiarised us with the kind of thought I am speaking of. People like Guénon, Coomaraswamy, and Marco Pallis use tradition in the sense of metaphysical knowledge revealed in an historical situation, of which every civilisation has its own branch and form and prophet.

I know I speak for many people, including myself, who find that the many occasional essays you've written in recent years have acted as a sort of bridge of access from the somewhat confined world of English literature—contemporary literature—to the bigger world of tradition, its symbols, its doctrines and myths, etc. Do you regard this work as of equal importance to your poetry?

No, in fact I don't. But it was work I had to do, not only as a piece of self-education, as it was when I began my studies on Blake, a sort of laying of the foundations, but for the reason you said, that one must provide a bridge of access of some kind. But, again, poetry is a living experience. These essays and works of scholarship, which have occupied a great deal of my time and have involved great labour, have in fact been works putting together the works of others, which is certainly relevant to the imaginative experience of poetry that I have tried to communicate. But, you see, that isn't a living speech. It has its value, but poetry is the thing itself. Poetry is the living language of living experience; poetry speaks from the soul, and that must always be a higher level than the other. But I must say that without laying these laborious foundations I don't think I could have written the poetry. This would have also been true of Yeats, who laid such laborious and firm foundations to his work, or indeed of William Blake, whom I found, to my surprise, was not the spontaneous visionary of the legend, but a most laborious student of the literature of tradition who laid his foundations with immense strength and care.

Your prose works do serve another purpose inasmuch as they are also a bridge of access to your poetry. A knowledge of your prose provides the supporting context to a reading of your poetry, so they have this double function, of leading to the larger world of tradition in general, and also of leading to your poetry.

Well, I hope that's true, because I often feel I should have written more poetry and less of this kind of scholarly labour that I've indulged in, but maybe I had to do this. It does rather seem to me that every poet of any quality is writing from deep studies of something or other. You can't just sit down and write poetry. A poet like Vernon Watkins had wide and deep foundations too. The trouble with many so-called poets nowadays is that they do not have this context out of which they are writing, so their work is very thin. It is only out of the day-to-day and immediate experience. No one studied these matters more deeply than Yeats did. I regret it in a way. I really think that it would have been better to entrust myself more to the springs of life and perhaps less to these other studies. But I'm glad you think it provides a bridge of access for people, at least on that level.

You would agree then, that for a poet of any imaginative depth at all, the modus operandi *of poetic vision is a mastery of symbol.*

Yes, most certainly. And when one has learnt the language of tradition, so to say, which is a symbolic language, one can tell instantly whether a given poet is writing with knowledge of this language or without. It isn't a different language for every poet that you read; it is one language that runs right through the whole of European and, to a certain extent, world literature. One knows immediately when a poet uses the symbol of water, or whatever it may be, whether it is being used with these resonances of meaning or without: Milton, Coleridge, Shelley, Keats, for example. To a certain extent Edwin Muir, Vernon Watkins. One knows that this is the language which is being used. Or one might find a similar word in some non-traditional poet like Auden, and one can tell immediately that it is not being used in this sense. One then experiences this as a loss of resonance. The mastery of a traditional language is of great importance.

What would you say is the purpose of symbolic discourse?

Symbols speak to the soul. The psyche doesn't think in words; it is the temporal man, the ego, that uses a verbal language. But a symbol which is finally grounded in nature reaches back to regions of experience that are far deeper than verbalization can ever reach. These symbols touch us at a much deeper level; they come from a deeper level and they speak to a deeper level. They strike these resonances. A symbol must be grounded in physical nature because that is where the form of the symbol comes from, but it also resonates in a vertical level, in the level of the soul, and possibly beyond that, again at a metaphysical level. Therefore, while words are, as it were, a horizontal level of discourse, symbols are a vertical level, calling into play all the different levels of our humanity: life, spirit, the whole range of our human being. Of course, dead symbols are not doing so; they are then like any other kind of verbalization. But when a symbol is living, it speaks to the whole being. And again, to return to Jung, whom I must defend, the soul receives its oracles in symbolic form, as for example in dreams, very seldom in verbal form, and more often visual than verbal.

Then the knowledge that symbols field is an aid to spiritual regeneration?

Certainly. It's an awakening. They are the strongest possible agents of what Plato calls *anamnesis,* the unforgetting, the awakening of that in us which, according to Plato, we know but don't in fact know we know. Because the symbol speaks to that level, it has a far greater power of awakening the inner dimensions, our inner being, than mere verbalizations which remain on the level of natural humanity living in a physical environment, the level of rational thought.

In a traditional society, symbolic knowledge gains its spiritual efficacy by being situated within a total metaphysical context.

Yes, if there ever were such a thing as this traditional society. I suspect it is an abstraction, that the situation is one that has never actually existed in any human society and is in reality simply the ideal point to which we refer ourselves. It does, of course, still exist for those who have understood and experienced in depth the symbols of any tradition, any religion. It is a possibility at all times, but a possibility for a whole society I should think never.

If we may take the example of Dante, for instance, he could rely, on the part of his reader, on the whole of scholastic cosmology so that when he used a traditional symbol that symbol resonated in his reader. Now obviously the modern poet doesn't have this supportive context, so when he uses a traditional symbol what can he really hope to sound in his reader?

In so far as he uses a traditional symbol that is part of a cultural inheritance, of course he can't sound anything, but in so far as the great symbols of tradition are themselves rooted in abiding reality itself, as light, water, the Great Mother, the Tree of Life, they come from human experience and they can speak again to human experience, if they are used with that intention. Yeats succeeded in using them in this way. But in so far as they belong to a cultural context, then, as we said earlier, I'm afraid the situation is very bad; they don't resonate.

Yes, it was this lack or this disappearance of a cultural context that concerned David Jones, wasn't it? I think it's this that makes him such a central figure in our time.

Yes, it concerned him very deeply. He did manage to use the Christian liturgy in a living way; he was probably the last great writer in this country who was able to do so. I think it would be impossible for someone like myself, for example, to do so, although indeed David Gascoyne has used many of the central Christian symbols with a tremendous resonance, though not in a liturgical context. In a way he's removed them from the liturgical context in order to use them with that sense of nowness which David Jones says is essential to any work of art. Yeats wrestled with this problem also, of what was available to him culturally. Of course he had Irish history, and Irish mythology to a certain extent. He used certain symbols like Leda and the Swan and gave them new power by his use of them. If these symbols are to be used it is for the poet to renew their power, as Rilke did, for example, with the symbol of angels, or Hölderlin with Greek mythology, or Shelley. The power can be renewed if the poet is great enough, and then this restores in some measure the past to the present. But merely to use them in a conventional manner expecting conventional response, that is no use at all; that's over. If the modern poet is doing so, it may well be that he is falling back not upon a living experience but upon book-learning, in which case the symbol is not alive in the poem to begin with, and therefore will not arouse any living response in the reader. Symbols are living things. I think Yeats understood very well that, as he puts it, 'Things thought too long can be no longer thought'. You can't go on repeating yourself, because art must always be new. If you are going to use a traditional symbol, it must come from the source of life itself; it mustn't only come from book-learning or it will be simply repeating something that had validity in the past. And that, far from renewing a symbol, is the surest way to kill it. That is why so many of the symbols have died. But when a poet can take a symbol, relive it, and restore it to its original glory by re-immersing it in the source of life itself, as I think Yeats does with Leda and the Swan, he brings it back into our experience and present in a living way.

In The Lion's Mouth *you have suggested that it may be that our times are sweeping away the concept of the cult as spiritual support. What, other than some form of idolatry, can you see replacing it?*

The cult practised unimaginatively *is* idolatry. What was expressed outwardly in the cult must be interiorised and experienced imaginatively. I'm afraid I can but give the answer that Blake gave, and that is that we must discover the God within, in the human Imagination. Instead of looking for outside supports, look within, for God is in every created being, in ourselves, in one another, in the whole of nature. Once we've realised that, the whole, apparently external, world becomes, as Blake says, 'one continuous vision of imagination', communicating at every moment its meaning. Immediately. When the sun rises, when a flower opens—all these are immediate communications of spiritual reality. That is an ideal situation, but I think we are forced into this situation by the fact that there's nowhere else to go except within. That is where we must go. This renews not only the inner world of dreams, which Jung very well understood, but it would have the effect also of renewing the outer world. When we experience the outer environment in a living way, it ceases to have this sort of inhuman deadness that it has for the materialist, and becomes in itself a living experience. Blake believed that poetry, music, and painting were man's three ways of conversing with Paradise that the flood has not swept away, that this is the voice of Imagination, that true art, which comes from the indwelling spirit of man, is the voice of God. The symbols presented to us in our own dreams and in our own living experience are living communications of the Divine. I know this is very dangerous. If one imagines, for example, taking the Christian Church out of our world, the prospect is very grim indeed. But Jesus himself taught that the Kingdom of Heaven is within, and I can only see, as Blake did, that this is the religion of Jesus. The Kingdom of Heaven is within and must be discovered by us there, not projected as formerly into sacred forms and sacred formulae, which indeed did serve to awaken the inner response but no longer do so and are therefore useless. It is only in so far as the outer forms awaken the inner realisation that they have any use; they have no other intrinsic validity. I can't see where else we can go, but I wouldn't want to be dogmatic on such an immense issue.

Would you agree that the erosion of spiritual boundaries that we see today can lead to the danger of arriving at a sort of neo-theism, devoid of the integral support of a specific tradition?

This is a great difficulty, but one must remember that symbols, wonderful as they are, are merely pointers that point towards realities. The things which are symbolised are enduring elements in human experience and in the cosmos itself and will not go away just because a certain symbolic language no longer serves to describe them. The realities abide. The God within is a living God, and every moment of our experience is just as close to the source as time past or time future. These things are realities; they are immediate. You may change the name, but you cannot remove the reality. You may abolish the cult of the Blessed Virgin Mary, but you will not by that undermine the reality of the Great Mother Goddess, the Feminine Principle, for whom the Blessed Virgin has stood for two thousand years as a valid symbol. She will be re-experienced; people will have dreams of her. I know people who have never been to church but who have had dreams of Jesus Christ, because the figure of Jesus Christ, again, is the central divine humanity, under whatever name, to which we are all as human beings oriented. We can entrust ourselves to the Real in the confidence that we cannot as human beings be totally removed from the source from which our life springs.

Of course, disbelief is another thing; it is a very regrettable situation in which the efficacy of the cult as a support for religious experience is removed from us. I quite agree with you that it is a very frightening prospect, but because the reality which was once mediated by the cult remains, we must not despair. I can only give Blake's answer, and indeed Yeats's, that rather than through the cult we can experience these realities through poetry and the arts. After all, the cult is itself a work of art, expressing certain imaginative experiences of a collective kind. It is a great mistake to think of the cult as being other than a great collective work of art. For example, the Cathedral of Chartres practically embodies the whole mystery of Christianity. You can call it a religious symbol; you can call it a work of art. There is no difference at that level. And art should itself be rooted in the spiritual and eternal world. When Blake seeks to say that art is religion, he did not mean at all that profane art can take the place of religion. He was trying to say that any supreme work of art is rooted in imaginative truth and revelation, and is in that sense fulfilling the role which cult and liturgy fulfil in ages which can make use of these. And Yeats, of course, who was not as good a Christian as Blake was, but was a deeply religious man, held the same. I know this answer isn't satisfactory but I think we have no alternative because the cult is going anyway. We know this. You and I have both, I'm sure, tried our best to make use of the cult and found it strangely irrelevant to our own deepest experience. And because we have no alternative, we are driven into seeking the God within; we have nowhere else to go.

On the basis of what you have said, can I now put to you a question which I feel is perhaps the most crucial of any that I've asked you this afternoon? If it is of the nature of symbols themselves that they have very specific psychological and religious connotations, and if one does away with the connotations when one does away with the cult, how can we use symbols at all without abandoning something of their real nature?

I'm afraid we're forced, however much we may try to escape, to the conclusion that we are living in the terminal phase of certainly a civilisation, and perhaps a whole world of civilisations. I remember Marco Pallis saying to me, when I made a bitter complaint about Christendom, Christianity as a cult, that I need not imagine that other religious traditions were in any better shape, that the same was in fact happening in India and in the Far East and in other places. And he said, I recall, that you can't expect anything else at the end of the Kali Yuga. And in this terminal situation, I think it is useless to try to keep alive the corpse of civilisation as we have known it. We have perhaps to undergo this spiritual death and rebirth. But one remembers the words of Jesus: 'Heaven and earth shall pass away, but my words shall not pass away'. The word, the *logos*, given to man, will endure as long as we ourselves endure. I see no alternative. Culturally, of course, I have to agree with you that there is very little hope. I wouldn't say no hope, because God has knowledge at his disposal that we ourselves lack. But in so far as I can see, speaking for myself, I see this as being the terminal phase of European Christendom—not of the teachings of Jesus Christ, but of the great culture, the cult, the whole story of man in the West for these two thousand years. I think it has reached its end.

You may have noticed that in my poems I rely more and more on nature, because I do truly believe in the words of the Jewish prayer, with which every Jew greets the day: 'Praise be to thee, King of the universe, who new createst thy world every morning'. So that is where I myself turn: it is to the immediate living experience of the living God, the God within humanity, whom Blake called 'Jesus the Imagination', by which he meant the *logos* within man. This was what Blake found to be the great difference between the Jewish tradition, whose conception is of a living God with whom man walks, communicating at every moment, to whom man is open and attentive, and the Greek tradition, which rather abstracts certain truths and sees reality as a great structure. When it comes to the final issue, all we have with certainty is the knowledge that our very existence rests upon the immediate creation of every moment that we live by this God within. And that comes down to the bare bones of things. At that point, which may be the death of culture and civilisation, there may be a rebirth in another dimension of which we as yet can see very little. All the poet can do is stand on the ground that remains.

The poet and artist do seem to keep the intuitive channels open at a time when, increasingly often, the sacred itself seems closed to both theology and philosophy alike.

There have always been the prophets as well as the priests, which perhaps Guénon and his school have somewhat forgotten. The prophetic spirit which 'bloweth where it listeth' is what Blake proclaimed, and he said that poet is only a modern word for prophet. And the prophets are those who speak for God. In other words, they speak not from the personal ego but from the Imagination which is the God within all humanity. This is still so. It seems to be what we are left with, taking the function of the poet in the deepest sense, spiritually understood to be the prophetic utterance. Yeats, you remember, says that genius is a crisis that unites the sleeping and the waking mind, that gives entrance to the other mind beyond the mind of the ego. In so far as the poet or the painter or the musician can keep open this channel through which the spirit speaks, things which we have not yet imagined, which we cannot know, the spirit, will speak to our age. There is always a message for every age. In that sense I am not despairing, as indeed it is not in the nature of the poet to despair of inspiration, because the reception of this spirit that blows where it listeth is precisely the task of any poet.

Who Speaks from the Dust?

SOME MONTHS BEFORE SHE DIED in 2003 Kathleen Raine remarked to me, 'It means nothing to be a poet in this country today'. This was said with a tone of voice such as one might use to declare an outcome of events to which one has no connection or interest. Given the relatively high public profile poetry now has, the poet's observation might appear to be something of a misperception. But it was meant as not so much an observation as a judgement. This poet had in her sights the type of poetry that is the natural expression of what she called 'quantitative culture': that is, demotic in spirit, individualistic in expression and materialist in its comprehension. At the beginning of her essay 'The Use of the Beautiful' the poet spoke of such verse as seeming

> to set itself no goal beyond description, sometimes pleasing, but just as often of displeasing things seen or felt. I doubt if anything is to be learned from such descriptions or from the self-expression of the subjective states reflected in so much current verse. Far from expanding our consciousness, we have often, on the contrary, in order to understand such states to makes ourselves smaller, like Alice, before we can get inside such mean rooms as are opened to us.

For Kathleen Raine, as for her master, William Blake, there was never any doubt as to what it takes to be a poet. 'One Power alone makes a poet—Imagination, The Divine Vision'. This stipulation is unconditional and proposes that the vocation of the poet is a very high one indeed. Could anything be more at odds with the conception of poetry so widely practised today? In the context of a culture that itself reflects the metaphysical depreciation of history, and which functions to all intents and purposes from within a worldview that has, over many centuries, gradually emptied out the natural world of its symbolic resonances, the defence of a metaphysical

39

poet's work must seem like a long-lost cause. Poetry now seems almost exclusively to be concerned with observing and recording private reactions to what is called 'the real world', a world for which any regard for metaphysical reality must seem like an obsolete attachment to the remote abstractions of prescientific speculation. But, as the poet records in her essay on John Donne, 'metaphysical . . . is a wholly misleading word. Metaphysical poetry is the least abstract, most concrete of all poetry'. What follows, then, might be thought of as an attempt to rehabilitate the validity of metaphysical poetry by means of an examination of the very heart of Kathleen Raine's imaginative vision.

At the beginning of her essay on Edwin Muir, the poet speaks of those 'accidental circumstances of the moment' that furnish something of the substance with which a poem is made. Such moments can, at the time of its creation, make a poem seem 'alive' and 'to the point'. But time itself can all too quickly diminish what once seemed a poem's very life-blood. Time, here as elsewhere, is an unsparing judge.

English poetry today seems largely wedded to the conviction that to record the ephemera of the commonplace is the natural and only substance of poetry. But to this poet, as she points out in her essay 'On the Symbol', 'nothing seems more unnatural in the art of poetry than "natural" diction, common speech, the conversational tone'.

In a little essay, 'The Writing of Poems', written in the early 1940s, the poet challenged this 'natural' way of conceiving poetry, which both springs from and leads to the 'wrong' way of writing poetry, which

> all poets know. It is the error of putting ideas into words. Only the poem can state itself, it is the thing in itself. To use the form of poetry as a way of paraphrasing some other truth, is to falsify . . . the error is in the way of living that such an approach to writing implies. That one should expect both to have an experience, and then to make a poem of it.

It must remain an open question whether, on every occasion, any poet could hope to measure up to the demands of the poetic vocation as Kathleen Raine conceived it—Kathleen herself being no exception; it is such a high ideal. That said, this passage is fully in accord with the poet's unequivocal vision of the imagination as a cognitive event that takes place above and beyond the commonplace.

The poet's belief was that the form (not the shape) of a poem is 'born from the Imagination', that 'legendary inspiration' from a transcendent source towards which the everyday self is rarely directed—that is why every thought has its own form. This was a poet always wary of the conventional notions of poetic structure: prosody, stanza, rhyme, and the like, holding them to be a fabrication—untrustworthy in so far as they might precede the authentic imaginative experience. In the same essay, we find: 'Poems are not made up. A fabric of words can be made up, but if it does not tell the truth the result is not a poem'. However, the poet did not believe that 'the truth for poets is anything less or anything different from truth in general'.

Later in the same essay we find a passage that gives more than a hint as to why her best poems, charged as they are with their characteristically luminous vision, are so often resistant to any sort of prose paraphrase. This is due to her insistence that the poem makes present an embodiment in words rather than a verbal imitation of something seen or felt.

> The poet is [not] a mere reporter and scribe of action, history or of nature itself. For poetry is itself one of the manifestations of life. A poem is the thing it states. It is the love, it is the history, it is the rose; it is the battlefield. The experience, the action, the landscape, the love, lives and is lived in the poem, not otherwise. The man who writes a poem lives his life in the poetry—and does not live that piece of his life, otherwise.

And then, as if to forestall any suggestion that the true poet inhabits some remote ivory tower, she goes on to say: 'Poets must not live apart in a private world. The poet must know humanity, history, love, hate, vulgarity and beauty, intimately and personally . . . but through and beyond himself the spirit of a poet must be entirely chaste'.

On reading such passages we should not conclude that the poet's view of the craft of poetry denies the importance of the technical demands poetry makes upon its creator. But we are obliged to have some understanding of the much wider context of the craft if we are to situate its effective place within the wholeness of vision the imaginative experience gives rise to. As the poet explained in the introduction to her first *Collected Poems* (1956):

> For the poet when he begins to write there is no poem, in the sense of a construction of words; and the concentration of the mind is upon something else, that precedes the words, and by which the words, as they are written, must constantly be checked and rectified. The critic need never raise his mind to this platonic idea at all, and sometimes verse is written by rules formulated by critics who have no knowledge of the laws to which the poet is subject. Such verse is not poetry, but an imitation of poetry. No poet will ever see reason for admiring even the most skilled imitator of the external form.

No doubt this characteristically uncompromising stance of a poet sure of the wellsprings of her vocation could sometimes be the cause of a certain neglect of technical polish in her poetry. But nowhere is there to be found a poem that attempts to succeed by technical excellence above all.

Rereading the essays that comprise *Defending Ancient Springs*, some fifty years after they were written, what must surely strike us now is how they are at one and the same time an impassioned defence of the highest values of the mind, and a lament for a unity of culture no longer possible. Indeed, such a unanimity of values it demands is inconceivable by the terms of that substitute for culture now so widely accepted. There is no need here to rehearse in detail the poet's rejection of this displacement of true culture; she has spoken amply enough in her essays of the terms on which her opposition rests. But in so far as it is applicable to a reading of her poems, clearly something must be said about those Ancient Springs from which she drew and with which she challenged the premises of the scientific rationale.

These springs are none other than the spiritual sources of that perennial wisdom in the form of metaphysical doctrine, archetypal myth and symbol, which are the various dialects of a universal discourse about the fundamental realities of Being and Intellect. By means of their analogical language, inconceivably deeper and wider in its penetration than any scientific account of reality, the eternal verities of Spirit can be known in states of being as living experience; an experience in which sensory, subtle and spiritual worlds, in their reciprocal unity, are mirrored in the realisable completeness of the human state. This analogical language articulates what might be thought of as the primordial tradition. The word 'tradition' here does not refer to historical continuity, but to an active realisation of what is in the beginning, not was in the beginning, since this is an eternal birth of the Spirit; the timeless emergence of the One that reveals to man the means to abide in that which is his true destiny and redemption. It may well be conceded that tradition will and does leave its traces through historical continuity (the arts are, after all, witness to this legacy), but in its essence tradition is beyond the world of time and space, as the space of a room is only made possible by the greater space that surrounds it.

In drawing as she did from the Ancient Springs of tradition, Kathleen Raine acknowledged realities of mind and spirit inadmissible to the materialist ideologies. As we shall see later in her poetry, to draw inspiration from tradition is to reject certain accretions and habits of mind with regard to the nature of perception and imagination. And to admit to this inspiration is to draw, ultimately, upon the traditional conception that the whole of the divine mystery is present in our very nature. And further, and particularly so for this poet, it is implicitly to affirm the immanence of the uncreated in the created. It is to make effectively present in analogical terms the transcendent in the actual, with the further implication that the 'natural'—the existential world of begetting and dying, of matter and its progeny—experienced without reference to anything beyond itself, is insufficient, even meaningless. This is the central 'illumination' of the poet's vision.

This 'illumination' inclines the reader's intuitive faculty, in the moment of contact with the poem, to recognise that the world of sensory perception is incomplete in virtue of the fact that it must rest upon something beyond itself, in the sense that the world of things that are perceptible must emerge from a world that cannot comprise 'things' or even 'thingness'. The materialist goal of attempting to arrive at an exhaustive account of the finite world—to grasp the created world in its entirety by empirical investigation—is doomed to failure as a comprehensive explanation of the Creation itself, since the indefinite extent of knowable things would demand that the investigator, in the words of Frithjof Schuon, 'multiply the senses exponentially'.

Yet a certain wholeness of comprehension is possible through the analogical discourse of imaginative vision. Such a vision does not diminish the creation to a web of empirical facts and statistics on the one hand, or illusion on the other, but envisages the full scope of its relative possibilities as being the expression of multiple states of being, where each level may evoke the divine principle as the source of its abiding reality. As the poet wrote in her essay 'On the Symbol', 'the language of analogy at once presupposes and establishes relations between different orders of the real, an orientation towards a source and a centre. The idea of the metaphysical is thus implicit in the very figures of symbolic discourse'.

On such terms as these the 'Divine Vision' proceeds. The task of the poet is not, as she points out in the same essay, 'the description of personal emotion, or the evocation of group emotion [as] is assumed by many writers of the present day', but to realise, in imaginative form, this orientation towards the sacred centre in all human experience. The poet is, however, no less an incarnate being than anyone else. The mutability of the perceptible world of every day is the poet's 'given', and all imaginative knowledge must be cast in the mould of its embodied forms. Poetry must present its imaginative vision through the context of the natural world, but must not devalue that context for its own personal ends. To do so would amount to a disruption of the efficacy of wonder to be an agent of the transcendent. We can hardly doubt that the star, the stone, the flower, that moved this poet to imaginative expression would be easily recognisable as such to you and me: and that the wonder they inspire is a moving experience held in common. But this making present of natural appearances in a poem must be done without betraying the function of imagination to transcribe the world of nature into the language of its noumenal source. We must not lose sight of the fact that, for this poet, the poetic art is, for both writer and reader, an exercise in the transformation of consciousness, an adjunct to contemplation of the eternity of the beautiful. As the poet noted in the introduction to her first *Collected Poems*, 'the ever-recurring forms of nature mirror eternal reality; the never-recurring productions of human history reflect only fallen man'. This distinction is fundamental to the poet's vision of her vocation. Like Coleridge, Kathleen Raine seems never to have regarded the senses as in any way the final criteria of our perception of the real.

Kathleen Raine was, of all things, learned in the historical legacy possessed by her belief in the timeless, all-inclusive vision that poetry demands. In her small monograph on Coleridge, she wrote:

a rediscovery of the true nature of poetry and a re-formulation
of the philosophy of the imagination which, deriving from
Plato, has fertilized every renaissance of European art ... [is] a
re-discovery and formulation of the true rules of poetry—
rules that can be followed, however, only by true poets ...
rules themselves inherent in the imaginative act, in the state
of passion, that demands a living participation of the whole
man that is not to be imitated by any merely mechanical technique.

In the opening of her essay 'On the Symbol', and in the section 'Fool's Paradise' in her *Autobiographies,* the poet gives an account of her perplexity at discovering, when she went up to Cambridge as an undergraduate intent on 'exploring the inexhaustible and lucid beauty of form and metamorphosis in nature', how outmoded the intuitions of her imaginative temperament seemed to her contemporaries. Beginning at the time of this 'confrontation', what she had, over many years, to come to terms with was a quantitative view of reality in which the purpose of knowledge itself excluded all qualitative resonances that, to the poet, gave the reality of the natural world its meaning and value. The quantitative view she found herself having to confront was in total contrast to the poet's actual experience—which was that the perceptible world is nothing less than a revelation of an order of truth and beauty beyond anything the empirical mind can conceive. In 'On the Symbol' the poet writes:

> When I was young, I looked for, and constantly discovered, the numinous in and through nature; and only in middle life did I first experience in an overwhelming degree one of these archetypal epiphanies. The vision was of the Tree of Life, with many associated symbols, all suddenly and clearly and simultaneously presented to my mind . . . an epiphany of knowledge, for these images are themselves the vehicles of that knowledge; only as such do they arise and exist. Their meaning is their only reality, the only content of their forms.

In so far as such a 'revelation'—that is surely the just word for it—is felt as lived experience and by the utmost mastery of art is embodied in words, poetry can be said to be truly 'personal'. That is to say, it is *of* a person and *for* a person in a way that cannot be adequately comprehended in empirical terms. It does not speak to some biological process or neurological circuitry. We do not fall in love with a process but as a person, with a person. As a person we experience a sense of wonder. At the passing of a loved one we grieve for the loss of a person, known more certainly in and beyond the normal intimacies of everyday life. The emptiness we experience at such times is that desolation of soul that is the loss of a connectedness with a person.

It is as a person we experience these qualitative states of being that open up to us an order of values and meanings beyond the processes of life that those values and meanings guide us through. It is this realm that the Divine Vision of the poet serves, in enabling us to see the world as a living epiphany—a vision of reality that entirely transcends any order of a supposed self-delusion: 'it is rather in a refusal or an inability to see what is before us that illusion lies', as the poet observed in her essay 'A Sense of Beauty', where she concludes that beauty is the real aspect of things, when seen aright and with the eyes of love.

Without doubt we are incarnate beings, so that the perceptible, embodied world is inescapably the given matrix of poetic language. But, uniquely, in our embodiment, we find it of our very nature to contemplate the origins and ends of things: to ask, to what purpose is there something rather than nothing? In pondering our destiny we cannot help but register the 'play' of things upon the senses and the mind, and in such 'play'—with the witness of the poet's visionary creativity—to become aware that we join with the divine in its 'play' at creating a world that so perfectly provides not only for a return of our responses to their origin, but also the intimations of the transcendent that will guide us on the journey. Such is the underlying metaphysical nature of Kathleen Raine's vision of the poet's vocation: a vision in which the divine act of creation coheres in the soul's apprehension of its mystery. How does this vision manifests itself in her poems?

⊕

A poem communicates person to person. An 'I' speaks to an 'I'. With descriptive poetry the poem registers a distance between the knower and the known. An object has been seen, an emotion felt, a thought registered. The polarity of subject and object is the structural foundation of the description; a subject has experience of something 'other'. But with the poetry that springs from Divine Vision things are not so straightforward. Take, for example, the poem 'Self'.

> Who am I, who
> Speaks from the dust,
> Who looks from the clay?
>
> Who hears
> For the mute stone,
> For fragile water feels
> With finger and bone?
>
> Who for the forest breathes the evening,
> Sees for the rose,

Who knows
What the bird sings?

Who am I, who for the sun fears
The demon dark,
In order holds
Atom and chaos?

Who out of nothing has gazed
On the beloved face?

Who is the subject here, and what is the object? What 'I' is address-
ing what 'I'? What is accounted for in these lines (that bear witness
to the characteristic visionary perception of our poet) requires the
reader to adopt a radically different conception of the customary
relationship between subject and object as it is usually configured in
common experience. Although it is not likely that it was known to
the poet, a passage from Eckhart's seventeenth sermon spells out
very clearly, albeit in theological terms, the metaphysical order of
cognition proposed in this poem (and in many others):

> In created things there is no truth. There is something which
> transcends the created being of the soul, not in contact with
> created things, which are nothing. . . . It is akin to the nature of
> deity, it is one in itself, and has nothing in common with
> anything. . . . It is a strange and desert place, too unnameable
> to name, too unknown to know. If you could annihilate your-
> self for an instant, indeed I say less than an instant, you would
> possess all that is in itself. . . . The Latin word *ego*, which means
> 'I', is proper to none but God in his oneness. The Latin word
> *vos* means 'you', you who are called to be one in unity. These
> two terms, *ego* and *vos*, I and you, thus both stand for unity.

The poem 'Self', in a series of questions, in effect collapses the
conventional assumptions about the relationship of subject to
object, dissolving the rigid demarcations that support the awareness
of common sense experience: the notion that such experience com-

prises a mind distinct and separate in its awareness of an object other than the subject who is aware. The poem thereby presents, in imaginative terms, the moment of intuitive experience in the soul in which things are known as they are in God (the eternity of the 'beloved face') who knows them into being by an act of self-externalization. In this intuitive moment comes the realisation that the poet's 'I' is none other than the 'I' who is all things in the divine unity.

This theme of divine identity recurs throughout the poems, as in, for instance, the last two lines of 'Named'.

> Yet by that unknown knower I am known
> And who I am.

Here, the poet records the moment of knowing as not being, by its very nature, available to reflective consciousness; being and knowing co-inhering in the experience of identity.

Earlier, I quoted a passage in which the poet spoke of the poem telling truth. In 'Self', truth is revealed, by a series of questions, to be how each observable minute particular, by the very nature of its knowable existence, is a mirror as it were of the 'no-thingness' of the wholeness and unity from which it springs.

'Self' is a relatively early poem. But the same metaphysical matrix of cognition and perception is evident in, for instance, the late 'Confessions', the first of which, tinged with a note of personal regret, reads

> Wanting to know all
> I overlooked each particle
> Containing the whole
> Unknowable.

In 'The Presence' the nature and location of the knowing 'I' is somewhat disconcertingly spread wide among the features of nature and personal memory. That is, until we realise that the knower speaks not from the standpoint of a separate, isolated perceiving ego, but as the focal point of a knowledge—heard as music—of the manifold realities that, in being perceived and memorised in the poet's consciousness, validate the poet's knowing the world as the externalisation of a shared unity of eternal consciousness.

The Presence

Present, ever-present presence,
Never have you not been
Here and now in every now and here,
And still you bring
From your treasury of colour, of light,
Of scents, of notes, the evening blackbird's song,
How clear among the green and fragrant leaves,
As in childhood always new, anew.
My hand that writes is ageing, but I too
Repeat only and again
The one human song, from memory
Of a joy, a mode
Not I but the music knows
That forms, informs us, utters with our voices
Concord of heaven and earth, of high and low, who are
That music of the spheres Pythagoras heard.
I, living, utter as the blackbird
In ignorance of what it tells, the undying voice.

Of the themes of the knowing 'I', and the One and the Many, there is, of course, a necessary coherence. The two themes are interwoven throughout the poems. Sometimes the one or the other predominates, but the two are never far from being mutually informing and illuminating. In 'Blue butterflies' eyed wings…' this coherence is given an especially delicate treatment: the poem is all the more effective for the fact that the reader has no need to draw any lines of thematic demarcation, so perfectly is the lyric moment caught.

Blue butterflies' eyed wings,
Eyed buzzard high in blue sky,
Mountain isles blue veiled

In fleeting shade of fleeting cloud,
Of these I am the I.

Given their metaphysical underpinnings, these lines are so much more than a mere imagistic triumph.

Section 6 of Kathleen's substantial 'Soliloquies upon Love' celebrates the inexhaustible catalogue of life, with a wide canvas that seems to take in, by its breadth, everything from the sublime to the banal, seen through the prism of Love both cosmic and human. Here, the poet brings the rich panoply of the created world to its point of origin, its *punctum*; that is, its native home:

Against immeasurable nothing stands the *fiat*
Of sun and the other stars, and the unfolding rose:
One point of life puts back all darkness.

There all is transparent, light runs through light,
Each mirrored in every other, all see themselves in all,
Every star is all stars and the sun, the small is great,
There none walks upon alien soil;
From far we look into that heaven by the lifting of the head.

This is to look into the eyes of Love itself, from the human perspective. In '*Amo Ergo Sum*', one of the poet's most loved poems, the poet enunciates the same theme, but from the perspective of the divine Love seen as the inspirer of the human heart in a state of wonder. The poem ends

Because I love
    There is a river flowing all night long.

Because I love
    All night the river flows into my sleep,
    Ten thousand living things are sleeping in my arms,
    And sleeping wake, and flowing are at rest.

We are reminded here of the poet's words, 'beauty is the real aspect of things, when seen aright with the eyes of love'.

References in the poems to 'the One', 'the Unknowable', 'the ever-present presence', 'the mystery' are hardly to some abstract, remote notion hovering in the penumbra of phantasy. Their subject is the preexistent context of all knowledge and experience. For the ancient springs of wisdom, nonspatial and nontemporal intuition is the condition of the interpretation of the space-time world itself. It is fundamental to the poet's vision, in terms of imaginative evocation, that in this intuition is the redemption of human perception and understanding as such. If this were not so, what would understanding *be*? Surely not simply a cognitive process activated to no end or to no purpose? This would be an outright contradiction of understanding as we experience it. To what purpose would truth ever be sought beyond perception, were perception all?

Remote as all this may seem to Kathleen's poetry, it is none the less fundamental to the implicit metaphysics of her imaginative symbolism. Without this metaphysical context, for instance, even a modest poem such as 'Babylon' would be incomprehensible:

> Not in vain
> This city where lost souls
> Hide and seek themselves—
> Great building-site of illusion
> Here and now always in us
> The divine for the divine seeking.

The same could be said of 'Say all is illusion…' At the other end of the scale, so to say, one of the poet's last poems, 'Millennial Hymn to the Lord Shiva', the calamitous error and waste of man's inhumanity to man and therefore to the planet, such as the poem catalogues as part and parcel of our phase of history, is seen as coming about as a result of our having lost contact with the redeeming holiness of the unknowable mystery as the source of all things. The poems ends,

> But great is the realm
> Of the world-creator,
> The world-sustainer
> From whom we come,

Who Speaks from the Dust?

In whom we move
And have our being,
About us, within us
The wonders of wisdom,
The trees and the fountains,
The stars and the mountains,
All the children of joy,
The loved and the known,
The unknowable mystery
To whom we return
Through the world-destroyer—
> Holy, holy
> At the end of the world
> The purging fire
> Of the purifier, the liberator!

At the end of time the destruction of the world returns itself to the holy mystery of the redeeming unknowable. In this redemption knowing is brought to its living reality, not remembered from past or anticipated in future experience, but to the eternal ground that is the absolute coincidence of being and knowing. This much the scope of the poet's imaginative vision implies in images of celebratory lyricism.

Just as the theologian might say that God 'knows' things into existence, including man himself, so the poet, in imitation, fashions images of existent things as making present their divine origin. The poem 'The Invisible Kingdom' ends:

Yet unceasing
The music of the spheres, the *magia* of light,
Spirit's self-knowledge in its flow
Imaging continually the all
Of which each moment is the presence
Telling itself to the listener, the seer in the heart

Contemplates in time's river
The ever-changing never-changing face.

This is an acknowledgement of the intimacy beyond division of subject and object, of that which is the intelligibility of things known. We can see with what skill the poet could conjure, in images of such delicate transparency, this momentous subject in 'Nature changes at the speed of life…':

> Nature changes at the speed of life
> From moment to moment, so that all,
> Bird, leaf and tree seem still, seem real, until
> We glimpse the conjuror at play—
> A dandelion's evanescent sphere
> Created itself, between yesterday and today
> Came, was, and is over, while I
> Marvel at the unseen geometer's skill
> Who builds the transience where we dwell.

All of which presupposes, as Eckhart reminds us, that at the root of the soul's knowing there is that which is not *of* the flux. This is the true 'I' who, in the timeless moment of knowing, is transfigured.

The all-informing light (that most apt of all symbols of the spirit) alluded to in poem after poem, is *the* moment of epiphany once granted the poet as entry to the world of eternity. It is the theme of 'That flash of joy…', for instance, but it makes its most explicit entry in part 4 of 'To the Sun':

> A hyacinth in a glass it was, on my working-table,
> Before my eyes opened beyond beauty light's pure living flow.
> 'It is I,' I knew, 'I am that flower, that light is I,
> Both seer and sight.'

This, surely, is Kathleen Raine keeping company with the likes of Vaughan and Traherne.

⊕

It is often said that the vocation of the poet is to bear witness. This witness, more often than not, has in view some social or personal aim. In this context, it is hoped, poetry is seen to possess powers of persuasion, an implicit capacity to effect some betterment to the fabric of living experience. Either that, or on a more personal level to offer a measure of solace against a rising tide of darkness that would all but overwhelm the inner light of conscience by which we, each, defend our interior, spiritual life. Can poetry go beyond the polar opposites of social and personal consolation? Can it bear witness to the supreme vocation of man in his integral wholeness and open up for his scrutiny those spiritual possibilities that seek to place the fulfilment of his existence beyond and above biological and historical process? Only rarely it seems, but as I hope I have shown, the poetry of Kathleen Raine is one such opening.

This is the ancient task of the arts, to be a support to contemplation of the eternal truths that frame our existence. It is to those truths that poetry must bear witness. In doing so it arrests what is fleeting, embodies what has no measure or duration, in order to make present a representation of the eternal spirit at the heart of creation. On such terms Kathleen Raine defends the Ancient Springs.

Epiphanies of Light

KATHLEEN RAINE'S POETIC VISION has two prevailing leitmotifs. By the inclination of the poet's temperament, it is a poetry of spiritual nostalgia (a quality it shares with the poetry of Edwin Muir) on the immemorial theme of the descent of the individual soul into the world of mundane generation. By instinct of vision it sees in the particularity of nature an image of the infinitude of the divine presence. The Judeo-Christian myth of the Fall, Plato's myth of the Cave, and the Neoplatonic myths of Demeter and Persephone especially, and of Cupid and Psyche might all be said to contribute to her imaginative themes, each in its way casting a luminous shadow over the poet's vision. The subtle contours of at least one of these mythical structures is hardly ever wholly absent from any poem.

This is not 'nature poetry'—outward appearances seen with eyes of flesh. Potency of image and depth of theme in this poetry appeal to powers beyond nature. Here, the poet's eye leaves the least trace possible of the psychology of the observer on what is observed. For all their incarnational qualities these poems seldom reconstruct a physical context between the seeing 'I' and its relationship with some observed scene, with all the psychological and optical continuities that such a relationship suggests in common experience. More often than not, nature is here presented as a series of 'snapshot' images: a tree, a bird, a stone, a shaft of light, with the immediate context or qualities described very often with the utmost brevity, as, for instance, in 'April's new apple buds':

> April's new apple buds on an old lichened tree;
> Slender shadows quiver, celandines burn in the orchard
>   grass—
> This moment's image.

or in 'That flash of joy—':

Like scent of budding leaves borne on the wind,
Or pure note, clear,
Heart trembles to, like water in a glass,
Like a flame that bows and leaps
As sound-waves pass . . .

Nature is perceived in the poet's eye as a series of individual points or nodes of cognition. Natural appearances do not stand as a reality outside and beyond the eye of the poet. Both nature and imagination are part of one and the same dynamic process. The perception of nature is not treated as a description of objects in physical space so much as a series of images invoking an inner, qualitative apprehension, each image gathering to itself something of the numinous presence of every image seen as a theophanic totality. For this poetry, such is the pattern whereby the divine principle is indwelling in each thing. The observer is thus the prefallen Adam or soul, the eternal moment of cognition at one with the essence of all named things. Each particle of nature's world, minute or vast, is itself the 'perfect signature' of what it is, while at the same time it is 'the everywhere and nowhere invisible door' opening onto the hidden presence beyond the threshold of being from whence we may discern and contemplate its sacred mystery. Thus the poet's eye does not look outwards into the distance of space in order to evoke or initiate the concatenation of semblances that nature 'seems' to be, but looks inwards with the eye of the heart to the qualitative space of imaginative perception, where nature's forms are the occasion for a recollection of their archetypes—their paradisal origin. Were it not for this transparency of phenomena, the theophany that is the world would be a totally bewildering prison of unintelligible multiplicity.

It is also important that we grasp the many modalities of the 'I' in these poems, for their boundaries and identities are ever shifting from poem to poem—even, on occasion, from line to line. Except where obviously autobiographical—the 'me', for instance, in 'Heirloom'—the 'I' of the poems is rarely that all too readily assumed 'ego' for, by the terms of the poet's imaginative vision, the 'ego' is no more than an inferred—'soul lonely comes and goes' ('Lachesis')—localisation of outward behaviour. As ego, the 'I' is unreal and unknowing as an individual identity. In which case, what degree of reality can be ascribed to that 'I' who is the poet? A question posed by this short poem:

> Do I imagine reality
> Or does the real imagine me?
> Unimaginable imaginer
> What part does the imagined play?

It is the omnipresent, omnimodal essence that is the theme, for instance, of 'The Poet Answers the Accuser' and of 'Dissolving Identity' (quoted below):

> As if permeable—it seems
> Body no longer bounds my times and places,
> Past and future merging in the measureless
> Abundance, not much or little, but all—
> Mountains, waterfalls, leaves, seas,
> Clouds, birds, skies, whatever is,
> The marvels of the shabby commonplace
> Suffice for the *mysterium* to indwell.

The ultimate reflecting surface of conscious perception that knows all that is known—'of these I am the I' ('Blue butterflies' eyed wings')—both makes knowledge possible and in 'Named' is the indefinable personhood of the soul: 'Yet by that unknown knower I am known / And who I am…' and in 'To the Sun' is all that is known:

> Who am I who see your light but the light I see,
> Held for a moment in the form I wear, your beams.

Finally, then, the soul's 'I am' is God's 'consciousness' that looks out at the providential 'good' of the Creation, as in 'Seventh Day':

> Every natural form, living and moving
> Delights these eyes that are no longer mine
> That open upon earth and sky pure vision.
> Nature sees, sees itself, is both seer and seen.

> This is the divine repose, that watches
> The ever-changing light and shadow, rock and sky
>   and ocean.

As the 'I' is specifically the organ of essential vision, it is the soul's apprehension of the world of creaturehood, the mundane realm whose vesture it has here donned. But it is also akin to a divine presence whose descent into Soul is to open the eye of cognition, so that when it is stirred by the diversity and riches of the outer world of appearances, the eye of Imagination perceives those outer appearances in the light of their original purity. For though the perceiver, like those souls enchained in Plato's Cave, is obliged to watch shadows only, those shadows are created by the light that gives them what substantial life they have—that one same light from which the soul itself descends and which is never entirely lost to its remembrance. The actions of the soul are by definition, and by the terms of the poet's imaginative vision, explicit qualities of cognition.

So, in the beginning, we open our eyes and are conscious of a 'reality' that invites us to know it. That is already the wonder of wonders, at once the profoundest mystery and the simplest action, as in the short poem:

> I've read all the books but one
> Only remains sacred: this
> Volume of wonders, open
> Always before my eyes.

This mystery, this act, addressed in part 4 of 'To the Sun', is already in some sense a state of illumination since it participates in the light of cognition that is not only the being of all we know but is also the light by which we know it:

> Nor that light is holy, but that the holy is the light—
> Only by seeing, by being, we know,
> Rapt, breath stilled, bliss of the heart.

Only the opacity of our habitual, bodily state prevents us from seeing the constant myriad epiphanies that comprise the book of nature—the world before us.

We are, then, caught in the pattern of a cosmic dream that dreams the soul's descent into that least substantial thing, the world perceived by a reflective consciousness, a theme perfectly encapsulated in this short poem:

> World:
> Image on water, waves
> Break and it is gone, yet
> It was.

From the deep interiority of the cosmic dreamer dream itself emanates to become the preformal essence of things; the 'thought' of the dream becomes a hidden language at the root of every named thing, whose meaning we are and whose ultimate significance, enquired of in these lines from 'Dream-Flowers', is the inscrutable light of the *logos*.

> There is a speech by none in this life spoken,
> Yet we the speakers, we the listeners seem;
> In that discourse, all signifies:
> But what mind means the meaning that then is known?

So it is, from the initial point of illumination there dawns a consciousness, an 'I' that knows, a creature of time, faced with the outward flow of nature's attractions themselves demanding to be recognised. In multiplicity the original one is compromised, is dismembered and scattered; essential unity is, in 'Natura Naturans', both veiled and revealed by the multiple and becomes movement:

> Veil upon veil
> Petal and shell and scale
> The dancer of the whirling dance lets fall.

> Visible veils the invisible
> Reveal, conceal
> In bodies that most resemble
> The fleeting mind of nature never still.

With the descent of the soul into the lower world there comes the burden of consciousness of self, the realisation that the world of multiple 'seeming' is but a shadowy replica of the paradisal world above, sullied by the presence of fallen man, as in the last section of 'Eileann Chanaidh':

> Because I see these mountains they are brought low,
> Because I drink these waters they are bitter,
> Because I tread these black rocks they are barren,
> Because I have found these islands they are lost;
> Upon seal and seabird dreaming their innocent world
> My shadow has fallen.

This is a poetry, then, not of what befalls the retina—a recording of Nature 'natured'—it is a vision of that abiding, invisible Natura concealed in every appearance, that insubstantial source of the original wonder. And yet, because it is no-'thing', this worldly habitation of the soul must be accorded the status of illusion, as in 'Say all is illusion…':

> Say all is illusion,
> Yet that nothing all
> This inexhaustible
> Treasury of seeming,
> The blackbird singing,
> The rain coming on,
> The leaves green,
> The rainbow appearing
> Reality or dream
> What difference? I have seen.

Only by way of this 'seeming' can we come to recognise the numinous presence that upholds what *is*! For what other reason should it *be* at all? We cannot come to know the Presence without first knowing the outward appearances of things, and we know it in such measure as we know ourselves, the agent of knowing itself—knower and known articulations of the one same reality.

This is the dramatic leitmotif of the poet's vision, the soul's fall from the paradisal vision of childhood innocence—its native Edenic realm—and not its exile in the domain where things are born, suffer and decay, this prison of generated nature where all is circumscribed by death. As so often in the poems—in 'Eudaimon' for instance—it is a matter of communication between the poet, the will of the soul, and her Daimon, the visionary inspiration of the soul's utterances.

> Bound and free,
> I to you, you to me,
> We parted at the gate
> Of childhood's house, I bound,
> You free to ebb and flow
> In that life-giving sea
> In whose dark womb
> I drowned.
>
> In a dark night
> In flight unbounded
> You bore me bound
> To my prison-house
> Whose window invisible bars
> From mine your world.

And so the soul comes to seem entirely claimed by the nature it has assumed in the existential flux, the 'natal waters' (in 'Message from Home') that all but submerge it. In rock, in flower, in wind, in the loved human face, enamoured of all these things in which it comes to recognise itself, it shares a common love that binds all things to one another—the theme of 'Message':

> Look, beloved child, into my eyes, see there
> Your self, mirrored in that living water
> From whose deep pools all images of earth are born.
> See, in the gaze that holds you dear
> All that you were, are, and shall be for ever.
> In recognition beyond time and seeming
> Love knows the face that each soul turns towards heaven.

The soul's love is not only a bond that unites all things. In each thing it sees itself as the underlying substance of that thing. It is a love that moves the soul to descend to the utmost particle of the mundane world, even to the point (in 'Exile') where it all but seems that the gulf dividing its own nature from what is 'other' is conquered:

> Their being is lovely, is love;
> And if my love could cross the desert self
> That lies between all that I am and all that is,
> They would forgive and bless.

The soul undertakes this radical descent or participation, so that a witness to the love that joins all things becomes evident, as in 'Message from Home':

> Of all created things the source is one,
> Simple, single as love; remember
> The cell and seed of life...

At the beginning of the poem it is spoken of as a knowledge of all things; the soul, being all that it knows, takes on the qualities of that which it knows:

> Do you remember, when you were first a child,
> Nothing in the world seemed strange to you?
> You perceived, for the first time, shapes already familiar,
> And seeing, you knew that you had always known
> The lichen on the rock, fern-leaves, the flowers of thyme,
> As if the elements newly met in your body,
> Caught up into the momentary vortex of your living
> Still kept the knowledge of a former state,
> In you retained recollection of cloud and ocean,
> The branching tree, the dancing flame.

So it is that the identity of the soul, within this alien abode, is never complete, never becomes total (in 'The Invisible Kingdom'), for it always retains some memory, some intimation of its origin beyond the play upon the senses that is the nature of sensory reality:

> We know more than we know
> Who see always the bewildering proliferating
> Multiplicity of the common show.

Yet it cannot escape the term of its exile among that which it also knows as an ensnaring illusion. For that reason it is subject to all the sufferings and perturbations of this labyrinth of darkness that is its mortal state. What the soul has knowledge of in its generated embodiment is just such as prevents its returning (in 'Yes, it is present all, always') to all that it originally is:

> ...these
> Blind, ignorant, sealed senses shut me
> From all I love, long for, know and am.

In the third of 'Three Poems of Incarnation', the soul's descent is spoken of as a transgression, as if against a mother's counsel not to trespass beyond the precincts of its true abode:

> Go back, my babe, to the vacant night
> For in this house dwell sin and hate
> On the verge of being.

But if soul does not descend how shall body be redeemed?

> I will not go back for hate or sin,
> I will not go back for sorrow or pain,
> For my true love mourns within
> On the threshold of night.

The poet's burden is to unfold the drama of the soul's trial of wandering within the kingdom of partial forgetfulness, of partial remembrance, of visionary occlusion, the accustomed sensory world that has powers of imprisonment to immerse the soul in a world alien to its original purity, an impediment that delays its return, as these lines from 'Story's End' show:

> O, I would tell soul's story to the end,
> Psyche on bruised feet walking the hard ways,
> The knives, the mountain of ice,
> Seeking her beloved through all the world,
> Remembering—until at last she knows
> Only that long ago she set out to find—
> But whom or in what place
> No longer has a name.
> So through life's long years she stumbles on
> From habit enduring all.

Implicit in this same delay of entanglement is the knowledge that the soul's mortal journey becomes itself a strand, a skein from which the fabric of suffering and joy, dark and light, birth and death, is woven. That is to say, perception itself takes on something of the veil of nature's appearances, itself puts on the fabric of illusion, for like is only known by like. Such is the theme of 'Into what pattern...':

> Into what pattern, into what music have the spheres whirled us,
> Of travelling light upon spindles of the stars wound us,
> The great winds upon the hills and in hollows swirled us,
> Into what currents the hollow waves and crested waters,
> Molten veins of ancestral rock wrought us
> In the caves, in the graves entangled the deep roots of us,
> Into what vesture of memories earth layer upon layer
>   enswathed us
> Of the ever-changing faces and phases
> Of the moon to be born, reborn, upborne, of sun-spun days
> Our arrivals assigned us, our times and our places,
> Sanctuaries for all love's meetings and partings, departings
> Healings and woundings and weepings and transfigurations?

No less part of the fabric are those other souls whom we have known and loved, partly known and partly caused to suffer in the blind search for identity, and who, in the knowing have become part of the one woven substance of all, as 'Threading my way...' tells:

> Threading my way, devious in its weaving
> Into the web of the world,
> Time's warp running from far back, and on
> Of lives, crossed life-lines, intercrossed, entangled,
> Knotted, knitted together, ravelled, unravelled,
> Hidden, re-emerging in new design,
> Always growing, unseen or seen
> Patterns we make with one another, distant
> Or near, from immemorial past
> Into unbounded future running unbroken,
> Threads so fine and subtle of lives
> We weave and interweave, slender as light,
> Intangible substance of the age-old
> Ever-extending all, makers and made
> Who feel the pull of love, of grief, on every thread.

The passage of 'time's warp' delays the soul's tread from ascending the path of return to its native realm. For the soul, time is the 'measure of absence' from the now-ever of its timeless self that is in turn the measure of the perpetual flux, the ever-weaving vesture of begetting and dying that offers no abiding sanctuary, as in 'The Halt':

> Travelling in trains of time, succession and causality
> From sleep to sleep, from dream to dream we pass,
> Desire from day to day drawing us on
> But never bringing to our abiding-place,
> For with our exiled selves we everywhere remain.

This 'absence' is not a measurable 'distance' that divides the soul from its native country. As spoken of in 'The Elementals', it is nothing other than 'a curtain, veil or door/A mist, a shadow, an image, or a world ... / ... through the thinnest surface', assuming 'guises and transformations', a procession of super-essential lights become corporeal, playing upon the surface of time.

The more we attempt to grasp this 'apparent' reality, the more paradoxical it becomes, for though it exists in time ever moving and changing, it never is any 'where' or 'when', so that the warp and woof of our perceptions in time, woven into the memories of what we recall, actually become the substance of that transient world—a world we make and remake in perception. Here is the theme in the third part of 'A Departure':

> It winds into the heart
> That unbroken thread
> From present to past,
> Without to within
> From seen to seer,
> Sky, garden, tree, bird
> Transmuted, transposed
> To memory, to pain
> . . .
> Become what I am
> Who am the sum
> Of all I have lost.
> Who am the maker,
> . . .
> I am my past
> And future approaching
> Days unknown.

But hidden in the very heart of each perception is that which is not subject to time's flow, is unmoving, is unconfined by time and place, indeed is that place (spoken of here in 'Monessie Gorge') where time is robed with living experience:

> 'I am the stream', I said:
> And yet not I the seer,
> The running water,
> The joy unbounded.

This, the still centre of our being, the Soul of the soul as it might be called, is the very condition of our witness of all manifestation and change: 'There is stone in me that knows stone' ('Rock'). It is the core of every perception that spans the measureless divide between future and past, that smallest aperture, the 'needle's eye' of the timeless that 'spans the heavens to find the punctum out' ('The Hollow Hill'). It is the axial root of being in 'The Elementals':

> From height to depth, circumference to centre
> The primal ray, axis of world's darkness
> Through all the planes of being.

That same axial ray of light sends an arrow of illumination into the heart of darkest matter. The *punctum* is in particular the 'moment', the ever-now eye-view of many of the poems, in which all things as distinctly perceived become part of the soul's living garment of experience, as in 'The Moment':

> To write down all I contain at this moment
> I would pour the desert through an hour-glass,
> The sea through a water-clock,
> Grain by grain and drop by drop
> Let in the trackless, measureless, mutable seas and sands.

That implicit order, the soul's true being, is imprinted in the shapes, patterns and rhythms of nature. It can be conceived as a series of archetypal forms that move through time-bound things, as a dynamic rhythm of energy that passes through the sea to shape the waves. Themselves unmanifest, the archetypes configure the proportions and qualities of manifest forms as 'shaped on the day of creation' ('Shells'). Their labour is to be 'ever the weaver of roses' ('Rose'). The soul's return is also, then, a return to an identity with the archetypal order, a restoration of 'one who before my days was beautiful' ('High Summer'): the beauty of earthly things is finally traced back to Beauty itself.

If its radical innocence is 'joy unbounded', what then is grief, the soul asks, for surely it is real? And what could it be but the pain of severance? For having come to know earthly desire, it must now relinquish its grasp upon what it has come to hold dear. Such love (in 'A Departure') has no choice but to embrace what it desires; the more desirable for the knowledge that the object of its love must pass away:

> 'It is their transience makes dear
> Places and days that once were home,
> Sheltering refuges of earth
> Nearest at heart when they are gone,
> Faces we do not see again;
> Is it not death that seals our love?'

Thus the soul gathers up the fragments of its mortal life, its temporary attachments made here on alien earth, in preparation for an ascent to the intelligible realm where the meaning and worth of their transience ultimately resides. In this realm—the abode of Demeter awaiting her Persephone—all souls are returned to the ever-present eternity of their being—from 'Monessie Gorge', again:

> Live on in me, remembered ones,
> I am your future and your memory
> Who, within this ever-moving now
> At rest in change, wore, as I wear,
> The seamless dress of earth and sea and sky.
> One in the long unbroken flow
> We who have been are one another for ever
> Whose voices to the stars must cry and cry
> In sorrow and in ecstasy, 'I am'.

Persephone returns to Demeter, which is to say the soul, now beyond time's depredations, is at one with its higher faculties and is thus able to perceive those mutable semblances it has left behind as presences 'with power, beauty and awe'; that is, in their 'abiding essences' ('The Elementals'). In terms of the poet's vision of nature, the journey of earthly travail ends at the point where the threshold of the soul's native country begins; end and beginning indivisible as a single point of numinous vision, as in 'The Return':

Epiphanies of Light

I have come back to ancient shores where it is always now.
The beautiful troubled waters breaking over the skerry
On the wind in spindrift blown like lifting hair,
Clouds gathering over the summits of Rhum in the clear blue
Are as they were
When long ago I went my way in sorrow.
Time, measure of absence, is not here.

The return is the soul's remembering itself back into its own essential being so that it may be more fully and abundantly itself after its confinement and its dispersal among the 'teeming myriad' seeming of the natural world. In terms of the poet's imaginative vision, we have to transpose the journey as one into the very heart of physical reality, for it is this poet's rare gift to speak of the timeless essences while holding on to a vision of nature that neither makes of it a remote abstraction nor finds in it an occasion for sentimental reverie. This is at all times a poetry of incarnation in which it is crucially important to acknowledge that in the soul's return to the paradisal state from whence it has fallen—which is also to say, in and through the spiritual cognition of nature—physical things of the sensory domain are not banished to some imagined limbo as if redundant and replaced by a new or alternative 'reality'. Here nature is redeemed *in its nature* by a fullness of vision that penetrates to the miraculous core of Being itself.

The thin veil of forms torn asunder, the bridge crossed from shadow to luminous source, the *re*-cognising of the mortal and natural as epiphanies of light—the simultaneity of all these is (in 'To the Sun'), finally, the art of self-identity:

Ancestral sun, do you remember us,
Children of light, who behold you with living eyes?
Are we as you, are you as we? It seems
As if you look down on us with living face:
Who am I who see your light but the light I see,
Held for a moment in the form I wear, your beams.
...

Presence, terrible theophany,
Am I in you, are you in me,
Infinite centre of your unbounded realm
Whose multitudes sing Holy, Holy, Holy?
Do you go into the dark, or I?

For the poet the question must remain. It was Yeats who said that
the saint goes to the centre but the poet stays at the circumference
where all things come round again. Kathleen Raine's poetic vision
embraces the sacred incarnation of nature as mirroring the holy
epiphany of the soul's intuitions. In the consonance of seer and seen
the poetic image here serves to express a vision that is at one and the
same time universal and particular, descriptive and analogical,
combining meticulous observation with precise invocation. The
immemoriality of her vision of the soul's function articulates what
the soul was created to know. Which is to say that the poet invokes
the more-than-human from the threshold of the human, as in 'The
poet is of those':

> The poet is of those
> Who see but cannot be
> In that holy place.
>
> Vision of mirage trembles
> In a dry wilderness
> Of an elsewhere island.
>
> Of garden and tree I have told,
> Mountain and clear stream,
> Remember, who may not enter
> That ever-present kingdom
> Where some I know and have known
> Have been and are always.
>
> Whose brightness from far away
> Shines on my desert journey:
> Yet I bear witness.

For what purpose the witness but to conjure a vision of the innate perfection of the unknowable on which all things rest? These poems celebrate the theophanic immediacy of truth and beauty present in the instantaneity of unencumbered perception. And the shadow also. For the absence of that purity of vision is the incompleteness of all worldly knowledge, the sorrow and distance of 'otherness' in human experience. When the purity of the soul's vision is restored, the nature of reality and the reality of our nature is nothing less than the face of the eternal spirit that looks out at us as we look into the panoply of wonders before our eyes—from 'The Invisible Kingdom':

> Yet unceasing
> The music of the spheres, the *magia* of light,
> Spirit's self-knowledge in its flow
>
> Imaging continually the all
> Of which each moment is the presence
> Telling itself to the listener, the seer in the heart
>
> Contemplates in time's river
> The ever-changing never-changing face.

In the final section of 'To the Sun' the poet describes the actual experience of her visionary intuition, an initiation that has proved to be the preformal mould into which by far the major part of her imaginative expression has been poured:

>   not in the seen but in the seer
> Epiphany of the commonplace.
> A hyacinth in a glass it was, on my working-table,
> Before my eyes opened beyond beauty light's pure living
>   flow.
> 'It is I,' I knew, 'I am that flower, that light is I,
> Both seer and sight.'
> Long ago, but for ever; for none can un-know
> Native Paradise in every blade of grass,

Pebble, and particle of dust, immaculate.
'It has been so and will be always', I knew,
No foulness, violence, ignorance of ours
Can defile that sacred source:
Why should I, one of light's innumerable multitude,
Fear in my unbecoming to be what for ever is?

Poetic Imagination
and the Vision of Reality

No one can doubt that the advent of modernist poetry introduced hitherto unexplored areas of creative expression. The sweep of its innovations allowed for an expansion of poetic vocabulary. New rhythmic possibilities were explored, and there was a move towards a diction that was closer to the cadences and usage of everyday living speech. But this ground was won at some cost. Beauty was certainly off the agenda. And the soul was more or less banished—made obsolete as a faculty of perception as materialist ideologies tightened their grip on all areas of intellectual enquiry.

As a result, perhaps the greatest loss was in a narrowing of the sphere of imagination, the soul's natural habitat. So effective was this curtailment of the soul's function that contemporary poetry has adopted as something of a norm the habit of assuming that it can do no more than speak from a presumption of reality that is limited to the outer world of sensory perception and its objects on the one hand, and on the other, as it were facing it, the inner world of personal emotion. These two domains, the one seemingly concrete and objective, the other a closed world of private feelings, the contemporary poet seeks to join through straightforward description of phenomenal reality or some form of subjective invention. Yet each remains cut off from the other by a gulf it cannot bridge.

And why not? it might be objected. These domains, after all, represent the world we inhabit and form the basis on which we communicate our experiences of it to each another. It is to speak of *a* reality held in common, without which communication would break down altogether. However, the limitations of such a view begin to be felt when we can grant that man possesses a soul whose organ of perception, Imagination, is an intuitive sense that there lies beyond the world of sensory experience an order of reality—ineffable, ultimately inexpressible—that is none the less the source of the incarnate world in all its reassuring solidity. This metaphysical intuition, native to our very being, when given a degree of realisation, can never accept that the world of sensory experience represents any sort of absolute reality. Even more: this intuition by its nature demands that we recognise that the essential condition of our worldly experience is illusory.

Historically, the poet, brother to the mystic, has an honoured place among those who have helped us to hold on to this vision of reality. It is the primary nature of poetry to offer us an imaginative re-creation of those interlocking orders of reality—the impalpable and the sensory—by which we come to understand the illusory nature of the sensory world. As the Vedantic doctrine of *māyā* teaches, it is not that the world is inexplicable, but that it is not self-explanatory. Quintessentially, the gift that is true poetic imagination is the ability to embody, as if seen from afar, what the mystic has experienced in a state of realisation. The primordial poetic utterance is one that offers us a vision of the world as an order of events that is ultimately indefinable. Which is nothing more nor less than to say that poetry reveals, by the use of symbols and in terms of imaginative experience, the structure of illusion. This is the paradox of poetic experience. It is what determines whether or not the poet is concerned with the revelation of truth.

The poet Kathleen Raine began early. She has recorded that, even before she could write, and seated on her mother's lap, she would speak her poems so that her mother could write them down. Notwithstanding a later qualification, that something of this poetry was first put into her head by her mother, what might we give to hear those poems now?

In the foreword to her final *Collected Poems* (compiled in her ninety-first year), the poet wrote 'that a writer's early work often contains the essence of the work that follows, a sort of map of that special vision'. We might expect, then, as we certainly find, that Kathleen Raine is a poet of continuities. Something of this is the subject of our present exploration.

Despite this early beginning, the poet did not publish her first volume, *Stone and Flower,* until her thirty-fifth year in 1943. These, and the poems of her next three collections, have remained among her most cherished and well known. The distinctive qualities of these 'early' poems were recognised and praised from the outset: their purity of diction using a relatively simple vocabulary; their often ambiguous, floating syntax; their powers of evocation over and above the descriptive; their absence of passive sentiment in ego-less vision in response to worldly experience, and, allied to this vision, an objective precision in the observation of natural objects (reflecting her early training as a botanist in the natural sciences). The poet's ability to invoke the cosmic dimension of love, self and nature was evident from the beginning, as was the way they 'hold' personal emotion in the natural object, thereby fixing the eternal in the transient. To these animating continuities she returned again and again. It is perhaps not so easy for us now to measure the impact such a vision made on her contemporaries, marking her out as an unprecedented, refreshing poetic voice.

In later life, when the poet came to reject many of these early poems, we can see that she was, by reducing their number, attempting to purge them of religiosity and emotional dross, the better to concentrate the authentic substance that was to be the lasting nourishment of her poetic vision.

In the very first poem of her first collection, 'Lyric', which remained the first poem of her final, chosen canon, we find incarnate that interpenetration of human and cosmic, spiritual and created universes that stamped her vision from first to last.

> A bird sings on a matin tree
> 'Once such a bird was I.'
>
> The sky's gaze says
> 'Remember your mother.'
>
> Seas, trees and voices cry
> 'Nature is your nature.'
>
> I reply
> 'I am what is not what it was.'
> Seas, trees, and bird, alas!
> Sea, tree, and bird was I.

Here, the natural object *is* the type of that instant of spiritual vision that gives rise to the poem. There is no hiatus of reflective consciousness to give admixture to the experience. In the last section of one of her last poems, 'Houseless hope…', it is no different.

> Joy, bird with no place of alighting, fly
> Through my sky's
> Infinite spaces, boundless
> Realms of delight,
> At rest in flight.

In the instantaneity of the imaginative experience, the warp and woof of opposites that is the cosmic fabric are miraculously woven together in the light of pure wonder.

Only rarely do any of the early poems extend beyond a single page. This is in keeping with the poet's practise at the time, of building a poem around just such a moment of spiritual identity, in which there is no expanse to allow a narrative theme to unfold. But this succinctness of expression amounts to more than simply a moment of identity. A characteristic of nearly all of her poetry is that it is centred on the immediacy of the moment of perception as an experience, in part, of the whole of reality. The fragment possesses the nature of the whole. In this moment of interaction in which the whole makes its presence felt is the token of the unity of experience with the Divine—the promise of our undivided life in the primacy of the Spirit. It is so in the early poem 'In the Beck'.

> There is a fish, that quivers in the pool,
> Itself a shadow, but its shadow, clear.
> Catch it again and again, it still is there.
>
> Against the flowing stream, its life keeps pace
> With death—the impulse and the flash of grace
> Hiding in its stillness, moves, to be motionless.
>
> No net will hold it—always it will return
> When the ripples settle, and the sand—

It lives unmoved, equated with the stream,
As flowers are fit for air, man for his dream.

It is so, still, in the late 'At the back-end of time…'

At the back-end of time
Leaf-fall of lives, dwindling of the great tree
To the acorn of forests, returning
To the nothing of all that is,
The seasons, the leaves, the loves,
Song to its source, soul to its star—
Winter's recollection of worlds to be.

The imaginative continuity of the poet's themes from first to last need not deflect us from recognising the differences in quality in the early and later poetry. We might note how, in the early lyrics, the implied motif of undivided, omnipresent presence is, as it were, more particularly incarnate in the succession of images. It is as if what was the emotional experience for these early poems is still a living impulse in the image. In the later poems it is more often the case that the lived experience has been reflected and recorded. This observation may be to make no judgement as to merit, but merely to acknowledge the difference of perspective as between formative poetic vision and the more nuanced apprehensions of mature perception. There is certainly no question that each of these different perspectives is meant to serve the ineffable wonder that is a recollection of the seamless unity of the Creation, however evanescent the instant of its embodiment. This is not to say the moment was 'unreal', for the moment *was*!

On what, we might ask, is the record of this present moment inscribed that it should be so inerasable? It is surely the living presence of that cosmic dream of the Divine Principle that weaves and unweaves worlds according to the laws of manifestation integral to the outward realisation of Itself through love.

This is the theme of that great poem 'Amo Ergo Sum' where the very formation of things coming into being so as to be discernible as objects of knowledge—through the human eye, itself miraculously part of the process—is celebrated as the beauty of natural events. Here is the latter part of the poem.

Because I love
> The iridescent shells upon the sand
> Take forms as fine and intricate as thought.

Because I love
> There is an invisible way across the sky,
> Birds travel by that way, the sun and moon
> And all the stars travel that path by night.

Because I love
> There is a river flowing all night long.

Because I love
> All night the river flows into my sleep,
> Ten thousand living things are sleeping in my arms,
> And sleeping wake, and flowing are at rest.

By means of its lyric intensity the poem fuses the domains of the natural and the supra-natural, making it impossible to distinguish between the nature of the observer and the thing observed. Each is subsumed in the being that is at once the particularity of the one who observes and the immanent presence of the Divine Person who is the source of the epiphanic moment of what is observed—the 'ecstasy-producing dance', as an earlier line of the poem has it.

The poem's refusal to identify the observer as an empirical ego greatly enlarges the field of possible vision. The restrictions of a private response to the experience of reality being removed, the intuition of belonging to the wider panoply of wonders that is the Divine Nature's inexhaustible fertility is given its proper estate. The radical boundary between mind and matter is dissolved in a recognition that both mind and matter are no more than inseparable modes of consciousness, a consciousness that is singular whatever its mode. The source is never possessed as if it were an instrument of the thinking, perceiving 'I'. Rather it is the modes that collectively possess the 'I' who, creating nature through the eyes of love, sees in the beauty of natural things the very essence of the ineffable reality that cannot be contained exclusively by manifest reality.

In the unassuming 'Afternoon sunlight plays...', the moment of wonder is caught without blemish.

> Afternoon sunlight plays
> Through trailing leaves I cannot see,
> Stirred by a little wind that mixes light and leaf
> To filter their quiet pattern on my floor.
> Not real, Plato said, the shadowy dancers,
> Imponderable
> Somewhere beyond, the light; but I am old,
> Content with these shadows of shadows that visit me,
> Present unsummoned, gone without stir.
>
> So angels, it may be.

Going from late to early we note once more the continuity of poetic vision between the lines above and these from the early poem beginning 'Not upon earth...':

> Not upon earth, as you suppose
> Tower these rocks that turn the wind,
> For on their summits angels stand.
>
> Nor from the earth these waters rise—
> To quench not thirst, but ecstasy
> The waterfall leaps from the sky.
>
> Those nameless clouds that storm and swirl
> About the mountain are the veil
> That from these sightless eyes shall fall
>
> When senses faint into the ground,
> And time and place go down the wind.

If in the early poems 'ego-less vision' is something of a confident assertion, in the later poems it is an article of faith and experience that underpins the familiar responses of many years of pondered experience. Yet it remains, on every occasion, a momentary realisation of an archetypal order of reality.

For all that, we are left with the paradox that the experience happens to a 'self'—the poet—a paradox that is solved only when we realise that this 'self' is itself a reflected moment of the all-enveloping indefinite number of localisations of the Divine Presence. It is the light of this archetypal order of the Infinite that casts, firstly, the 'shadows' of manifest existence that are natural phenomena that then, secondarily, themselves cast shadows within their own order of manifest reality.

The poet has, at this point, the symbolism of the shadows on the wall of the Platonic Cave, as it were, deep in her poetic blood. This blood-line runs deep and widely in her expression of the subtle interplay that perception and reality exchange. It colours the distinctive tone of her perceptive vision, as it animates the structure of her imagination.

All evidence points to the fact that these poetic images are not 'abstract' any more than they are simply emotional analogues. Were it not so then we would have to conclude that these are poems in which a flight of personal fancy has been allowed to build insubstantial mansions in the air. Not to acknowledge the operative presence of the Platonic symbolism as the implied ground on which the poet's imagination builds, diminishes our appreciation of what gives these poems their vital breath. It is to miss the significance of the specificity of the poet's references to the natural order. For these are never objects that know only the laws of biological process, of birth and decay, measurable things to weigh and dissect. Tree, stone, star, shell, fish, rock, rain, wind, each is, in the light of the poet's perception—itself a spark of light struck from the Infinite—a world-image of wonder. As such they are powers that of necessity have a cause that is other than their effects; a source in the ineffable 'beyond'. These, the final lines of the early poem 'Seed' tell us that this is so.

External and innate dimensions hold
The living forms, but not the force of life;
For that interior and holy tree
That in the heart of hearts outlives the world
Spreads earthly shade into eternity.

In this last line, we note how the poet's authenticity of vision allows her to reverse the direction from which the Platonic light flows—the inverted symbol being all the more effective for its imaginative daring.

The 'Three Poems on Illusion' are central to the poet's achievement. They would be unthinkable without the effective resonances that accrue to an imaginative vision that registers the objects of nature as intimations of the soul's immersion in a world where the rigorous division of subject from object is refused by the experience of being 'at one with nature'. In the intuition of interpenetrating orders of reality lies the key to why nature can lift our perception beyond the merely human, to find its identity in the uncreated and undying as it is reflected in the transience of nature's protean life-cycle. 'The Instrument', the second of the set of three poems, ends:

And it may be that soul extends
Organs of sense
Tuned to waves here scarcely heard, or only
Heard distantly in dreams,
Worlds other otherwise than as stars,
Asteroids and suns are distant, in natural space.
The supersonic voices of angels reach us
Even now, and we touch one another
Sometimes, in love, with hands that are not hands,
With immaterial substance, with a body
Of interfusing thought, a living eye,
Spirit that passes unhindered through walls of stone
And walks upon those waves that we call ocean.

Towards the end of her long life the poet wrote many short poems—haiku-like in their brevity, but having for all that expansive reverberations. She once told me that she thought these were her lasting contribution to the formal possibilities of English poetry. In many of these brief, condensed poems the interplay of the real and the illusory reaches a level of sophistication such that the poet's art is perfectly submerged in the artlessness that is that art's true mastery. In the first of the 'Short Poems 1994', the archetypal reality becomes totally translucent in order to affirm how its 'nothingness' is none the less the measure by which the least instant of any one thing is granted its existence:

> Against the *nihil*
> One candle-flame, one blade of grass,
> One thought suffices
> To affirm all.

In the second of this series of eight poems, the poet in old age is forced to acknowledge that after all the possible attachments the soul may make with the objects of sense, there comes a bodily death such as will challenge and disabuse the soul of these false identifications.

> Time to unknow
> What has been known,
> Time to undo
> What has been done—
> What will remain?
> The naked soul
> To judgement come.

In yet another, the fifth, the poet's legacy to the reader is an offering of her life's imaginative work, a gift open only to those who have access to the one same identity we share, beyond possession, in the eternal order of the permanently Real.

> All I have known and been
> I bequeath to whoever
> Can decipher my poem.

If we are to avoid the error of thinking that the poet's use of natural imagery loses the identity of self to biological process, then we must grasp a further implication inherent in her deployment of these images. Here, it is all to their purpose that the poems convey to the reader, through emotional nuance based on sharply focused observation, something of the ineffable truth of the poet's inspiration, and how this relates to the technique of poetry-making.

In response to a questionnaire on rhyme in *Agenda* in 1991, the poet made it clear that she thought matters of poetic technique in general are determined in advance of poetic utterance by the level of reality that informs the imagination—prose and free-verse being, as she says, 'appropriate to the natural mind, rhythm and rhyme to the formal genius of the soul ("For soul is form and does the body make"—Spenser) and to what the modern poets never mention, inspiration'.

Given that the poet would certainly include herself among the poets of inspired Imagination, at first sight this might seem somewhat at odds with the fact that in her own practise she seldom used traditional, formal verse structures. Her rejection of full rhymes, she confesses, revealingly, is 'because the rhymes impose a kind of affirmative confidence proper to another experience, when life was full of certainties, religious ... or the over-confidence in their own culture of Dryden and Pope'. However, it becomes clear that for her the matter is more complex, for the question of form relates to the poet's level of consciousness. It is a question of that 'inner music' that causes the soul to 'dance' when a state of 'enhanced consciousness' is attained, so that the form of the poem is determined by a pre-existing music or rhythm. This 'vertical' conception is very different from the horizontal continuities of past practise in which shape is superimposed on word patterns in the light of an established precedent. Needless to say we are here as far away as it is possible to be from the assumptions that inform the freedoms of *vers libre*, whose demotic manner proceeds from, in this poet's eyes, 'the materialist ideologies of the modern West'. Such freedoms assume, consciously or otherwise, that, as she says, 'there is only one level of consciousness'. All of which seems to imply that the poet thought of the necessary formalities of poetry-making as discovering and revealing in the fusion of diction, image and symbol, the true cadence inherent in the emotion of any given poem's subject matter. The poet concludes, 'The clearer the imaginative perception, the surer the form ... the serious task of the poets ... is to illuminate the world with glimpses of beauty and meaning as these are known to the soul. Sorrow and joy, and the sound-current of the universe, which is music and dance'.

This is exactly what we find in that early, inimitable masterpiece 'The World', with its simple, repeating vocabulary, spare, cyclical diction and skilful evasion of a regular poetic form. The poem presents an unforgettable vision of the cosmic genesis' emergence from the measureless, eternal *punctum*—the birth point of the world from transcendent nonbeing.

> It burns in the void
> Nothing upholds it
> Still it travels.
>
> Travelling the void
> Upheld by burning
> Nothing is still.
>
> Burning it travels
> The void upholds it
> Still it is nothing.
>
> Nothing it travels
> A burning void
> Upheld by stillness.

Maintaining our hold upon the poet's continuities, and turning to the late 'Wisdom of Words', we find the deeper breath and swell of the poem's longer lines flowing outward from that same *punctum*—which is here, additionally, the poet's 'pen-point', tracing its way across the written page—to encompass the whole multitude of wonders that comprises the world as well as all that the 'heart has known'. The poem ends:

From word to word I trace my way, seeking, divining
Scarcely discernible messages, passing
From life to life clarities, marvels, epiphanies
All hearts, all souls have sought,
Bringing to my moment all those who once were, have
    dreamed,
Have known and praised, have sung, have cried aloud.

Cosmic music of water and wind and stars
Flows on for ever, but this human realm
Of meaning, none knows but we,
These memories, told and retold, imparted
From dream to dreamer by such as I,
Whose only knowledge is what we have made to be.

Let these lines lead us back to one more of the poet's continu-
ities—the place of the human heart, its voices, its pulses, its places,
its loves; even, at times, as the seat of evil—in so far as these are
instrumental in giving us a more complete knowledge of the right-
ful meaning of the substance of the cosmic fabric.

Through the medium of the soul's language that is human
speech, the heart of love is revealed by the poet to be at one with all
that lives and breathes as knowable nature. The heart is then the
vital repository of all that is veiled from mere eyes of flesh. The task
of the poet is to marry, by naming, each object to the essence of love
that is its immortal birth. In the coming and going of the seasons, in
the interval of bud to leaf-fall, the rise and fall of the tides, in the
heart's systole and diastole, the one undying rhythm marks out the
pulse of the Creation. Here is the theme radiantly expressed, albeit
in the shadow of war, ending the early poem, 'Passion':

The sky said to my soul, 'You have what you desire.

'Know now that you are born along with these
Clouds, winds, and stars, and ever-moving seas
And forest dwellers. This your nature is.

Lift up your heart again without fear,
Sleep in the tomb, or breathe the living air,
This world you with the flower and with the tiger share.'

Then I saw every visible substance turn
Into immortal, every cell new born
Burned with the holy fire of passion.

This world I saw as on her judgment day
When the war ends, and the sky rolls away,
And all is light, love and eternity.

Again and again in the poems, human love is seen not only and simply as a reflection of the Divine Love, but as being, in that, subject to the joys, the rigours, the desolations and the estrangements of the divisiveness (male/female) that the human heart is heir to. This, the soul's journey on earth, is most fully explored in the long sequence that is *On a Deserted Shore*. But this accomplishment, unsurpassed of its kind, is more than worthy of our full attention. The following study attempts to give it the honour it deserves.

In the early, modest 'Woman to Lover', the eternal feminine that is the heart's resonating love-object is identified as being wholly absorbed in the elements of the created world, as if to remind the lover of the extent of love's common source in the Creator's love of his Creation. Much of the evocative power of this deceptively small lyric is in the way this subject-object relationship is transposed to the human couple and suggested only by silent implication. This true identification of Love's source is required by the very nature of human love which, if it is to bear its fullest meaning, must be understood in a context that relates to it beyond the passions of human sexuality. For the nature of love is ultimately cosmic. A man and a woman in love rehearse the reciprocal, generative rhythm of the Universe.

In this poem we find an intimation of the theme that, as we have seen, is the poet's presiding continuity: that a full understanding of human experience requires a larger vision of what connotes reality than that afforded by the world of fugitive, perishable mortality. In this poem in particular, the lover is invited to understand his love of a woman as part of the interweaving of the total cosmic projection, where it alone endures in an order of reality itself loved into being by the Divine Presence. Here is the poem.

> I am fire
> Stilled to water,
>
> A wave
> Lifting from the abyss.
>
> In my veins
> The moon-drawn tide rises
> Into a tree of flowers
> Scattered in sea-foam.
>
> I am air
> Caught in a net,
>
> The prophetic bird
> That sings in a reflected sky,
>
> I am a dream before nothingness,
> I am a crown of stars,
> I am the way to die.

Undoubtedly, in the later poems there is an accounting of the heart's enrichments and failings. This is especially so in the poems of *The Oracle in the Heart* of 1980, where the theme of self-reckoning is the dominant mood. The record is unflinching, even at times harrowing, as it is written out in the poems and was lived out in the pages of life. In the self-accounting that is the occasion of 'In My Seventieth Year', the poet sees herself as the medium of the *Logos*—'I myself a spoken word'—that one 'majestic voice' that 'raised me to life' and thereby set her upon the journey of her life. The poem speaks, then, not only of an empirical self whose mortality suffers and undergoes the experiences of a life lived, but also from the vantage point of that Self of all 'selves', a presence

Consubstantial with the earth,
Contemporaneous with the stars,
With the sun that lights the world,
Morning and night of the one day
In which I walk today, all days.

This poses the question of the authenticity of the identity of the self to whom the voice of poetic utterance belongs; the identity that, in its time, has been called upon to record the ongoing passage of life towards death. To what extent is the poet responsible for the 'burden' of suffering caused by the self—seeing that the poem is cast in that light—by the interweaving 'of good and evil, time and place'; all the sustaining opposites that are the generation of life as it is lived? The poem resolves its dilemmas by retracing the origins of the heart's loves.

Though not explicit in the poem, we infer the contextual motif from earlier poems. The shadow serves in so far as it registers the light's presence. If what is known is that alone which is loved, then failure to love is an unknowing, for only in the light of love does anything realise its essential perfection. Failure to love is here a failure of knowledge, that ever-present context of the earthly experience—a failing whose burden we perpetuate rather more than we amend. The final responsibility for the failures of the heart must be weighed from within the context (with all the moral difficulties this may pose) in which the Author of the light is ultimately also the Author of the shadow. The heart of the individual we are created to be is part only of the great unfolding drama of the cosmic dream that is, as the poem has it, 'earth's great cry of joy and woe'—that consummation of the cycle of the All-Possible that 'must be/Before the concord can be full'. As part only of the larger whole it is not given to the individual to weigh and judge the final outcome of the greater pattern of possibilities—always and ever the dilemma of moral judgement. Without evil and injustice, goodness and equity would lack occasion to be exercised and so would not exist. The poem ends,

Shall we condemn what has been made,
Who makes this world and calls it good,

Amends and heals through endless time?
All that I have done amiss
All that I have failed to be,
Since he creates he must forgive,
Since he has made me he must love,
For I am but his act and will,
Who framed me both to give and bear
The wounds and sorrows of the world.

In the final analysis, only the Saint, in perfect knowledge of the Real, possesses perfect love—*is* perfect love. As the poet succinctly records in the brief 'Soliloquies':

To make the imperfect perfect
It is enough to love it.

And this by no means rules out 'A saint's certainty respecting the unsure' in 'Paradox'.

⊕

In the way that it is love in all its modes that threads together the strands of the poet's experience in the earlier poems, so it is time that becomes the backdrop that unifies the world of human experience in many of the later poems. This gradual transmutation of imaginative context culminates in the poet's last substantial poem, 'Millennial Hymn to the Lord Shiva'. This is surely a latter-day genuflection in the direction of Yeats's 'The Second Coming' in so far as it answers to the destructive powers that must emerge at the extinction of a civilisation—this last now more certain to us than to Yeats. However, the Hymn, with its sometimes faltering rhythms and prosaic inventories, is not the poem where the theme of time is most profoundly embodied—even if it is the poem that most emphatically states the cosmic necessity for the intervention of time's end to be 'the destroyer, / The liberator, the purifier' of the fruits of human conduct.

In the substantial, three-part 'Hymn to Time', the multiple levels of reality that are manifest by the very nature of time are explored in the light of the poet's past personal life. Here, time's ever-flowing current is the engendering medium that conjures the seeming world of nature, as well as the domain of human imagining. As a seamless experience it is honoured by the poet as being the repository of the 'treasury' of memories—the making of a life recalled in wonder. But that same wonder reveals time, 'whose now is unending', to be the instrument of beyond-time, around which the forces of creation and destruction revolve. This moment, never part of the action, is the absolver of all personal actions and their outcome, as each moment, mirrored in time, repeats the eternal patterns of love and pain brought to consciousness in the very fleetingness of the passing of their enactment.

At the centre of this never-ending interweaving of the experiences of love, pain, time, memory, is the knower, the identity, the witness who never surrenders to the changes of time, and so knows all that once was and all that is to come—to whom no moment is lost. Here are the final lines of the first of the poems:

> Now without end or beginning Time
> With your long necklace of skulls, who will add mine
> To your tally of lives, each rich in its infinite present,
> Nothing, take as you will all that was once ours
> As from moment to moment, day to day
> All that for ever is passes before us,
> Will ever not have been once and for ever.

Indeed, this identity of Self with the timeless moment is the sole guarantor of the reality of the experience in consciousness. Where else could the event be so inscribed but on its pages—'where life's a dream / Of profound untellable mysteries'—if it were itself the subject of constant flux?

Something of the same theme spills over into 'Fire', the following poem of the canon, where the interplay of the known and the unknown is captured in a meditation in praise of the nature of fire. Firstly, that of the 'Beautiful, flickering, translucent flame' of the familiar hearth coals that return to the poet's present moment of contemplation the 'carboniferous forests' of past millennia 'where none ever walked'. In the act of burning in the grate the coals transform one worldly element into another. Next is fire as the embodiment of the world's living, principal substance, that in returning all to ash produces a 'constant light' whose rays might 'blaze / Into such a star' as would 'comfort us with infinite forgiveness' of our undoing.

Finally, there is fire as liberator from all that is the subject of impermanent reality. By its abiding measure alone, whatever is created of the sorrows and joys, the loves and losses that make and unmake human worlds, there is redemption by reabsorption into the Divine Principle—source and nature of all. The poems ends:

> Fire, subtle undoer, loosener of bonds,
> Free, you are the freer
> Of all that is destructible, perishable, but we
> By flame cannot be burned, nor can you consume away
> The intangible thought I offer you in praise
> As you roar in glory through houses and worlds and universes
> Turning our dust to stars.

So we conclude. In examining the thematic continuities that form the central ground of Kathleen Raine's poetry, we find that a full appreciation calls for a recognition that the soul remains the proper organ of perception of the Real in all the multiplicity of its modes. Only in this, the 'soul's native place', is the depth and complexity of human identity and knowledge found to have its fullest and most valid meaning. As the means of imaginative vision, the symbolic discourse of the soul is the essence of poetic expression. Against the diminishments of modernism, Kathleen Raine has left us a body of poetry that affirms the perennial teaching that true poetic vision is an imaginative re-creation of the inexhaustible ways in which the perception of reality is necessarily permeated by the Divine Presence—a Presence without which that reality simply would not be.

That Dream Is All I Am

For we can unsuppose Heaven and Earth and annihilate the world
in our imagination, but the place where they stood will remain
behind, and we cannot unsuppose or annihilate that, do what we
can. Which without us is the chamber of our infinite treasures,
and within us the repository and recipient of them.

THOMAS TRAHERNE

WRITTEN IN THE SPACE OF TWO WEEKS IN 1972, the 'long' poem
made up of 130 short poems, with an additional poem at both the
beginning and the end of the sequence, comprises Kathleen Raine's
On a Deserted Shore. This part-elegy, part-tribute, a meditation on
the spectrum from joy to grief of a love found and lost through
death, seems to have attracted little appreciative or critical attention
despite its obviously being a poem of major stature: 'Better than *In
Memoriam*', the poet confided to me—which gives the reader an
idea of the poem's status, at least in the eyes of its author. Some-
thing of the poem's neglect can no doubt be attributed to the very
terms by which it deals with the subject of love: such terms as are
seldom met with in modern poetry.

A sequence certainly, but not with a conventional, linear develop-
ment. No two poems are consecutive, but a reading of the whole
communicates a powerful sense that each poem is intimately inter-
connected with each of the others. Each poem relates to a common
and orientating centre as it is reflected at a turning periphery. Noth-
ing develops, and there is no cumulative climax in the conventional
sense. The last poem is in the same relationship to the overall theme
of the sequence—the 'event' of love—as is the first. Each poem
might be thought of as the momentary illumination of a multi-fac-
eted object turning in a beam of light.

The sequence is a dialogue, perhaps without precedent, between
poet and beloved where the beloved is never felt to be present as a

discernible individual, except in the special sense that he is present *as* the features of the natural world.

> You who cast no shadow, nowhere, everywhere,
> All that you loved you are,
> Sun's gold on the sea, waves far out from the shore,
> Flowing for ever. (114)

That the inspiration for the sequence was the poet's relationship with Gavin Maxwell some years earlier is knowledge that has to be imported from outside the poems themselves. If it was vital information, the poems would surely make more of it. There is little in the form and content of the poems (Sandaig and Eriskay and 'the rowan tree' are mentioned only in passing) to suggest that such knowledge is essential to an appreciation of them.

Cloud, hill, stone, tree, flower, shore, flowing water are addressed by the poet and seem themselves, as what they are, to address the poet in return. The dialogue explores the theme of love from the perspective of the poet who, after the death of the beloved, is left to live out the balance of life alone in the world of time's passing. But it is more than that, for these are poems that reach out to a conception of love in a wider cosmic context, a context that does not allow of any disguise of the extremes of grief, paradox and redemption that the most profound love engages—indeed, they celebrate them. The presence throughout of the beloved, as mediated in the landscape and as of the landscape, lends a tone of objectivity to the poems that might at first make them seem remote and detached should the reader be expecting a higher degree of emotional involvement in this poetic territory. Added to this is the marked absence of any erotic element. Syntax and diction specifically heighten the overall sense of objectivity, as we shall see.

By contrast, one of the subtlest features of the sequence is to grant to the soul—the place where the event of love is enacted[†]—a status

---

[†] Of considerable relevance to any understanding of the location in which the vision of the sequence is enacted is the poet's confession: 'I have never identified myself with England or English poetry. I have always felt it was another country, a

that is almost autonomous, as if it possesses values in isolation from the everyday human context of love. A mark of this tendency is the way in which objective and subjective poles of experience seem so frequently to dissolve or blur. Thus it is that the flowing of the spirit creates, shapes and disperses the continuity of the poet's experience.

> Heart's truth: a moment out of time,
> Pollen-grain adrift,
> How small and fine,
> Golden upon the spirit's breath
> Into that quiet chamber sown. (94)

Here, as so often, there is a mastery of intuitive knowledge at work, a sense of the poet's making a record of emotional experiences that all but defy apprehension as distinct, comprehensible thoughts. All of which might mistakenly be taken to indicate that the poems are overly abstract: not so. Reading them should suffice to convince the reader that these poems are shaped from their initial stimulus in a profoundly felt personal experience.

That the 'event' of love is, in the poems, enacted ultimately within a cosmic context in no way obscures the fact that the sequence explores a failed love, an unrequited love (perhaps), even an impossible love. Elements of all of these are present as surely as it is evident that the poet has drawn upon her own dreams in the making of the sequence. We are at the same time led beyond a simply human frame of reference as we move through the poems. The phrase 'cosmic context' is no figure of speech here. The implied setting of the theme is that human love is a distant reverberation of the fact that, since God loved the world into being, we, as created in His image, in the state of love recall the presence of the divine.

It becomes clear that this cosmic context of love instates a bond between temporal and eternal states of being. The entire sequence recognises that the imperfect, bounded joy that is human love is, in

foreign country at the other side of the border.' See 'Kathleen Raine Interviewed by Joy Hendry', *Agenda* 31:4/32:1 (Winter–Spring 1994), 56–93: p. 58.

reality, the presence of a lost, unbounded paradise whose mirror image in this world is the sorrow of love's human impermanence.

> Not sorrow breaks the heart
> But an imagined joy
> So dear it cannot be
> But we have elsewhere known
> The lost estate we mourn. (111)

The finite state of personal love is inescapable just as, equally, the power of love to inspire a longing for union with the illimitable source of Love itself is felt with heightened immediacy in the state of being in love. But the poet is here in exile. From whence comes this sense of alienation, which accompanies the experience of love in a world no longer the habitation of the beloved? Poem 82 locates the source unequivocally.

> Original sin:
> I stand condemned, being born,
> To cast the human shadow;
> We darken each our sun,
> Who have not done, but are, that wrong.

Thus, we are in the presence of the basic paradox that underpins the sequence. In being created we are as a shadow to the light of our eternal birth; we are the 'wrong' that occasions our human insufficiency, itself the seat and origin of our grief and suffering. Against this there is certainly the implication throughout that not to love, not to be in a state of love, is a form of spiritual death: it is to be, in a sense, unreal.

Yet there is that which permits some reclamation of what is lost in this spiritual death. In the solely human we are distanced from the illumination of the spirit that is none the less awakened in us by love. In love itself the poet is attracted and summoned to the source of light by its least manifestation. With what notable precision, as well as concision, is light, source of being, transcendent and immanent, remote and immediate, evoked in the thirteen words that are poem 123.

Ah near at heart:
Far star's reflection in a well
Is still
Light.

The most challenging aspect of the underlying paradox is that love
is the experience of the intensely personal, yet can be the passage to
the transcendent and the eternal.

In love the bound is able to embrace and savour the unbound. To
be cooped up, as it were, in loveless experience is to know that the
world and our place in it is as a prison.

This empty world too small,
Heart's void too great,
Everywhere visible the wall,
Nowhere the gate. (88)

All such experience takes place in the soul, which is where the con-
traries of the human state make their presence felt as the undertak-
ing of a hazardous journey: love, sorrow, joy, grief are present in the
human heart—the organ that is their 'place'—as various fates
encountered on the path to the soul's destiny.

Where my treasure is
A grave:
My heart also
Empty.
                    Sorrow
Is its own place, a glass
Of memories and dreams; a pool
Of tears. Narcissus pale
Sees his own drowning face. (1)

In some of the poems sorrow is not only a sentiment felt by the poet
at the loss of love, but also the acknowledgement of a hidden power
to recover to some degree the boundless, uncorrupted place of love's
origin.

> Sea-change:
> The grain of pain
> Love layer on layer enspheres;
> Sorrow its gradual pearl
> Perfects with life-long toil
> Beneath the tides. (65)

In a world in which all is transitory, love's sorrow is inevitably ('love is born to grief', 110) embedded in unstable emotional experience. The ebb and flow of the tides at the behest of time, is as of love's ordeal. Despite a rather ungainly second line, in these lines the movement of the sea has the symbolic adequacy of an element in whose immensity, constant flux and shifting moods—'moil' elsewhere—there is none the less the possibility of renewal in the at times despairing, at times hopeful, emotional ebb and flow of love.

⊕

To return to the marked absence of the 'person' who is the object of the poet's love: such references as there are to 'dear friend' (67), 'you', 'man of light' (79), and so on, are rare and in any case hardly serve to make present in any immediate sense the object of such a pronounced devotion. This is only puzzling (if that) until the reader comes to acknowledge that the poems, in their imaginative intensity, are primarily a series of meditations on the state of love itself. We might recall the poet's words: 'The experience, the action, the landscape, the love, lives and is lived in the poem, not otherwise . . . The man who writes a poem lives his life in the poetry—and does not live that piece of his life, otherwise'.

And yet, the beloved is often spectrally present in being recalled to memory. Memory, the poet must concede, however it may recall direct experience, has no power to bring back the actual experience of love: another of its sorrows.

> Memories: shrivelled leaves
> To keep or throw away.
> Love cannot piece by piece
> Remake the felled tree. (84)

Memory, throughout the sequence, relates to immediate experience as to an object apart from that experience, possessing once a living immediacy, now severed from the vital root that gave it a meaningful life in this world.

> From your grave-side
> All ways lead away,
> And time is long, my love,
> And memories fade,
> Old hearts grow cold:
> Must I too break faith
> With joy? (85)

Again, as so often, the poem closes with a question: in contemplative vision the imperatives of resolute action are suspended.

In being true to the experience of love, these poems make little attempt to re-live or illustrate the exchanges of what might more familiarly be described as a 'relationship'. As already observed, the erotic makes no sort of appearance here. This being so, and in being all but absent as a person, the beloved makes little direct contribution to the emotional tension of the poems. This, when coupled with the imagery drawn from nature that embodies the poet's love, objectivizes the imaginative intensity of the sequence. This is evident in the following beautiful lines, in which a union of the lovers beyond time and place is powerfully evoked by becoming, precisely, pure imagery.

> In your boundless state
> All night afloat
> On lift and fall of the great sea
> Rocks in the bay my anchored boat. (100)

Such memory states are akin to dream states in which the intimacy of union is all the more total since in the dream, dreamed and dreamer are one and the same: such is the intimacy so often contemplated here, poem by poem.

⊕

The intensity of the sequence does indeed demand a slow and contemplative reading. It is undoubtedly the case that the distilled essence that is the distinctive hallmark of these poems, with their resonant suggestibility, is sometimes achieved by way of a syntactical complexity. This may have acted as a bar to a wider appreciation of the sequence. Be that as it may, such complexities in this case offer no more (rather less) resistance than the modernist innovations found in Pound, Eliot and David Jones, for example. All that is needed to construe the meaning of any poem is present in the poem itself. This is not to imply that the challenge is inevitably negative. Surely something of what is needed to address the complexities of an imaginative theme of this scale and depth will necessarily be embedded in a degree of linguistic complexity: specifically in the frequent concision of the poem's syntax, as can be seen in several of the poems quoted. It would be perfectly possible to recast such poems to bring them closer to a prose order of sense; but what would be lost? In making such a change, it would be the reader's loss not to notice and acknowledge the mastery with which the complex interplay (one might even say 'entanglement') of syntax with cadence tellingly articulates that of past, present and future orders of the temporal process, with the multiple states of being in which love immerses its participants. Moreover, this interplay can be seen to recapitulate the poet's questioning exploration of her emotional themes. The contemplative pace of a reading is often signalled by the fact that many of the poems have a dash or colon at the end of the first line. This is usually a short statement or naming followed in subsequent lines by an unpacking of the thematic implications buried in the naming. Such poetic techniques are used with a subtle mastery; never more so, for instance, than in these lines where imagery and syntax intertwine, one about the other, to hold the emotional experience in place for the reader's contemplation.

> Grief's metamorphoses:
> Anguish, small pregnant seed,
> Becomes a worm that gnaws through years,

At last quiescent lies; not dead;
Till waking, what winged impulse takes the skies? (109)

One of the most recurrent images in the sequence is that of 'house' and, related to it, 'place'. To speak of the 'cosmic context' of love that is at the meditative heart of the poems is to suggest, perhaps, something shapeless, a distancing from the personal immediacy that is the experience of love. But for all the undoubted vastness of the contemplative resonances of the poetic landscape, there is a balancing intimacy at work; a sense of meaningful locality; of lived familiarity.

Significantly, in the opening poem, 'sorrow' (to become a leitmotiv of the sequence) is allotted 'its own place, a glass/Of memories and dreams'. In poem 6,

> Home is the sum of all
> The days that sheltered us;

while in 87 the 'unvisited house' of the beloved is beyond the barred gates of 'memory', the key to which, for 'Some' (the poet is equivocal here), unlocks the way to 'the grave, Paradise'. And in 106, with intimations of a once familiar dwelling, the 'small house of life' inhabited by the poet is contained in the immensity of the 'Great . . . domain of love' that encompasses it: a beautiful evocation of the expansion of emotional and imaginative life that love visits so vitally on those who live its condition.

> Great the domain of love:
> Farther than love can see
> From my small house of life
> Realms of your new state encompass me.

The memorable lines of 128 capture with distilled precision the simultaneous sense of a living participation with the familiar, the tangible, as being experienced within a sense of the unworldly, detached condition that is the emotional volition of memory and dream.

Opening a vanished door
I move on insubstantial feet
About your window, desk and chair,
Reviving each familiar object there.
Do memories of the living build
Memory-houses of the dead,
A place at heart where we may meet?

Once again a poem ends on a question in recognition that in the emotional ambience of love, the boundaries and divisions of common experience lose something of their directive influence.

Above all it is the familiar features of a place once shared that are the habitation of the poet's soul as much as they are the 'person' who is the poet's beloved. Time and again it is these features that anchor by analogy the lover's mutable states, giving a familiar locality to the emotional substance of the poet's meditations. In the third poem of the sequence, for instance, the soul of the lover wanders through a landscape that both reflects and *is* the shaping of the poet's experience.

I hid my heart
Within a certain stone
In a far mountain burn,
World-egg in its blue shell,
Invulnerable until
That pebble crushed,
Power and life were gone:
Not where we live but where we love, the soul.

This last line, besides being a translation of the Latin epigraph (from Erasmus) at the head of the sequence, in addition affirms a basic principle of the cosmology of the sequence as a whole. The world is not an empty existential space waiting to be inhabited by our presence and actions; it is the internal space of our experience, a space that is only ultimately made real and valid within the eyes of love: else it is a mortal prison. Poet and beloved are not in space, space is in them and of them as a vital order of consciousness that recognises the numinous reality to which love is present. (This is the explicit theme of the poet's earlier 'Amo Ergo Sum'.)

To inhabit this space is to be free from 'This body's clay' (79), the 'body's blindfold' (72), since

> Longing of lips and thighs—
> . . .
> The language of the flesh
> Too faintly cries. (46)

The mortal body is the seat of desires and appetites more commonly the spur to passion than to love, and as such a repository of deceptions that mask, even destroy, that deeper involvement with the soul where are found the timeless springs of abiding love.

> Flash again, golden wing,
> Across my sterile plot,
> Seeking in vain
> Similitude of glade and dell.
> Where human passions dwell
> Few flowers spring,
> Too far from that remembered hill. (80)

The sense of a localised, specific place as the habitation of the soul's reflections is present in one of the most subtly focused of the poems. Here the interfusion of imagery drawn—we are convinced—from an actual scene, reflected in the surface of a lake, furnishes the inverted context of the poet's darkening experience of love; a place whose colouring and contours, none the less, provide the authentic site of the soul's misgivings.

> Shadow of hills on the still loch, mysterious
> Inviolate green land, whose sun is cool as water,
> Whose stones bruise not,
> Seems soul's native place, this weary road
> The dark country in a glass. (78)

Such inverted shadowlands—'You who cast no shadow, nowhere, everywhere'—as the natural world provides are everywhere invoked in the sequence as the ordained environment whereby the soul's trials and tribulations, inherent in the living experience of love, are marked out. All that is bound by place, whether it be mortal body or nature in the widest sense, is none other than an ordering of Spirit— the integral background, beyond life and death, of the soul's earthly life. It is by the measure of Spirit that the poet acknowledges at one and the same time the inescapability as well as the insufficiency of an existence that merely 'comes in life and goes in death' (5).

> Downcast on the ground,
> The form of spirit
> We are but do not know
> Save by a shadow
> Distorted, earthbound. (113)

That all forms of life, all the travails of the soul, are but the movement of Spirit, a reflection in the temporal of an eternal state of being, order and bliss, runs throughout to make its final appearance in the address (a moment of epiphany) to the beloved that is the last poem that frames the entire sequence. It ends:

> *I saw for a moment as you might*
> *These sheltering boughs of spirit in its flight.*
> *Shall you and I, in all the journeyings of soul,*
> *Remember the rowan tree, the waterfall?*

How poignant, that final question.

⊕

Night, and its accompanying stars, feature in many of the poems; both, by their very nature, conveying a much less immediate and localised sense of place. Even before the sequence begins, the preceding poem signals the importance of night and stars as circumscribing the boundaries of human and natural worlds as well as indicating the presence of the dimensionless world of the soul's habitation that is beyond specific denotation.

> *The faint stars said,*
> *'Our distances of night,*
> *These wastes of space,*
> *Sight can in an instant cross,*
>
> *But who has passed*
> *On soul's dark flight*
> *Journeys beyond*
> *The flash of our light.'*
>
> *I said, 'Whence he is travelling*
> *Let no heart's grief of mine*
> *Draw back a thought*
> *To these dim skies,*
>
> *Nor human tears*
> *Drench those wings that pass,*
> *Freed from earth's weight*
> *And the wheel of stars.'*

Night and the stars form a curtain screening from direct perception the lost paradise whose radiance is yet seen in the starlight that studs the dark veil of night. What is beyond remains hidden but that there is a vital reality on the other side of the curtain is known only to intuitive knowledge, the imagination that love energizes and informs.

The 'Strange bird' flying 'across my evening sky' of 47 becomes emblematic of the soul's wandering through the placeless night, which for that reason can offer no sanctuary. The 'certainty of strong desire' needs must find a place of fulfilment, but the soul/bird's flight is here 'traceless' in 'harbourless night'. Because the dark curtain of night is the interface between bound and boundless worlds it can be taken to connote an indefinite realm between fallen and unfallen worlds. With this understanding we see that it is the

mercy of starlight to project from the unfallen world no pronounce-
ment on human failing.

> Out of the arms of night
> None can fall,
> Refuge of sinners
> Whose merciful stars towards us
> Beam from their height
> Indifference
> Absolving all. (103)

The potential of the hidden world to influence the manifest world is
also explored. The traditional, alchemical symbolism of the inver-
sion of the two orders of reality, whereby what is above is mirrored
in what is below, is invoked in 77, where the movement of the 'danc-
ing stars' is the dynamic pattern of the movement of earth's ele-
ments as they shape the inherent structures of natural growth.

> Arid bilbergia's rigid leaves
> Describe each its parabola. Slow the flow
> Water takes from air, air from swirling space,
> Comes to its term, to standstill dies.
> As above, so below,
> Traced by figures of the dancing stars.

One of the most telling of the poetic evocations of the symbolism
of the star occurs in lines where its appearance, by being held back
to the last word of the poem, is all the more striking and significant.
Yet this is no actual star, but its mirrored image in the heart—a
marker of the depredations of the passage of time in a love that had
once regained its paradisal state. These lines recall the unity of love
where poet and beloved are oblivious to any future loss their very
mortality must incur in the time-bound world.

> Time was
> When each to other was a glass,
> And I in you and you in me beheld

> Lost Paradise,
> With every tree and bird so clear
> Regained it seemed:
> We did not guess how far
> From the heart's mirror the reflected star. (51)

From the outset it is clear that these are poems built out of a recognition that shifting and inter-penetrating states of being can be made, through natural imagery, to reflect and embody a meditation on the many facets that the experience of love presents. Here nature—both creative and created, the one permeable by the other, fused but not confused—speaks, the one to the other, to enact a reciprocity of emotional recollection and defining image. Whether it is a matter of the cosmic mystery of love, or the lover's acknowledgement of the joys and sorrows of love on a personal level, these are seen by the poet in terms of the emotional resonances of natural scenes and objects that are an imaginative re-casting of the participation of love. This is touchingly illustrated when the poem explores states that would be, according to common sense, mutually exclusive. In 126 the poet intuitively recognises the beloved as being located in the dream state, yet also finds him present in the perception of natural objects.

> Whisperer in the wind—
> From what dream do you look upon this shore
> Grown strange and fair and far?
> Rain walks with heavier tread,
> In rustle of grass you are,
> Then not.

Elsewhere, this permeability of worlds is movingly evoked in lines where the poet is wholly identified with the dream state, since the state of love most faithfully portrays the dream that is her entire being, all the poet has ever been and is.

> Say I must recognise
> I but imagined love

> Where no love was,
> Say all is a dream
> In whose brief span
> Childhood, womanhood, the grave
> Where my love lies:
> That dream is all I am. (53)

The dream state is taken as analogous with the state of being in love throughout the sequence.

When the beloved has passed to the 'beyond', whether in dream or death, whose barred gates (67) would seem to offer no possibility of contact, it is the dream state that none the less allows a degree of communication. The poet may reach out through thought and word to address the beloved who cannot respond in kind. But since both were, in the past, part of the same all-encompassing dream that is love itself, both are in the poet's present state of reverie, through the features of a landscape once familiar to them both, united again.

> We who from day to day depart
> From the country of the heart
> In death return
> To the fields our feet have travelled, our tears sown:
> Sleeper beneath the rowan tree,
> You have become your dream,
> Sky, shore, and silver sea. (12)

In 18 the individual dreams of poet and lover were once 'Interwoven in one world'. Now, through death, the 'invisible sanctuary' that was that interweaving is destroyed, leaving only sorrow as the poet's refuge.

> No title mine to mourn—
> From my own memories exiled
> Since you on later friends bestowed
> Those regions of your dreams and mine
> Interwoven in one world.

That finespun texture rent,
Invisible sanctuary torn down,
Where but in sorrow shall I hide?

Again, negatively, in 68 the dream state offers no comfort and no path of return. The same negativity prevails in 121.

Somewhere, it seems,
You who walk with me in sleep;
But in the sand of dreams
Your passing leaves no trace
To follow or find that place.

But the purity as well as the sorrow of the dream of love are linked in 33, where the poet juxtaposes the beauty of the world, formed from the 'unfallen' *fons et origo*—to the lovers a seeming 'ancient dream'—with the poet's sorrow, death transforming the mirror of nature to 'an empty glass'.

Perhaps the least substantial hold on any state of reality in the dream of love becomes in 64 sufficient for the poet to conjecture a reunion at the end of all possible realities.

Image of an image, shade of shade,
In memory or dream,
Time future or time past,
In this or any world or state of being,
Shall we who parted
Meet at last?

Finally on this theme, in the lines of all but suppressed sorrow that are 45, the timeless state of the dream of love, once shared, has become in this world the very state of the wounded pilgrim (the poet), who walks alone the path of time willingly as the destined outcome of having embraced love itself.

For the beat of a heart
A world, a dream endures,

Yet on this earth we met,
And every stone is dear
That wounds love's pilgrim feet
Walking the way of time's
Six thousand years.

Throughout the whole sequence the journey of the exiled soul is undertaken with a richly nuanced sorrow.

These poems capture, with an unfolding succinctness, the sense of how the experience of love may profoundly transmute and imbue the perception of a world whose significance might otherwise seem diminishingly limited to time's transient momentum. Part of their quality and accomplishment is how they challenge us to spend time (if needed) construing their complex distillation. In so doing we are moved not only to a deeper appreciation of the poetic stature of the sequence, but also to its unique celebration of seldom approached dimensions of the states of love.

That Wondrous Pattern

NOT EVERY POET IS A PROLIFIC ESSAYIST, or even a writer of prose, but when a poet does write on other poets and on poetry in particular, even if not their own, it is as well to turn our attention to what they have to say. At the very least, it is more than likely that we will find there some guidance as to what forms the context of the unspoken assumptions that have informed the poet's practise. Those very assumptions are, after all, the fertile soil into which the imagination sinks its roots. Such guidance is made all the more necessary when the vision of the poet in question runs counter to the expectations of the reader, referring as that vision may to areas of thought and knowledge that are unfamiliar to prevailing currents of literary value: even going so far as to challenge the very mental premises of the age to which they are addressed.

It is also likely that we will find in such essays a more explicit unveiling of those hidden assumptions as they inform the life-blood of the poet's imaginative energies, being there in a way more didactic than is appropriate to the more symbolic resonances of metaphor and analogy in poetry. Such is the case with the work of Kathleen Raine.

$$\oplus$$

We are in need of a counterbalance. In a world that is in relentless pursuit of a quantitative evaluation of everything, an age that has forgotten that a phenomenal world necessarily entails a noumenal that is transcendent to it—a recognition that every existent being is the effect of a preceding cause—there must arise from time to time a voice to reaffirm the timeless, universal order that relates the one world to the other: joins the realm of ultimate principles to the manifest world where we find the embodied wisdom of our imaginative life in which things are known *sub specie aeternitatis*.

To read Kathleen Raine's essays is to find oneself negotiating a spiritual and intellectual landscape far removed from the preoccupations of what we currently think of as 'culture': those diminishing returns of 'self-expression' we call 'art', sustained by a new elite of purveyors and explainers of banality, anxious to convince us of its superiority to our common-sense reaction, in the face of it, of uncomprehending bewilderment. For this 'culture', the imaginative arts are limited to the expression of the mundane through personal emotion as having an exclusive claim to be the substance of art. What has become entrenched is the idea that the arts can no longer meaningfully relate to anything beyond such evidence as the senses might suggest. This follows from what has been the cumulative acceptance, based on the material sciences, that reality is in essence quantitative and that any appeal to a higher order of thought is at best mistaken, at worst amounts to a subversive heresy. It is a type of prejudice that chooses to ignore the obvious fact that it is in the intuition of conscious awareness, not itself available to scrutiny by means of reason or sensory knowledge, that we know all that we can know, and in which all things possess any reality they can be said to possess. All these diminishments Kathleen Raine's essays challenge head on.

How has this narrowing of the possible accomplishment of the arts as a depository of beauty and wisdom come about? In keeping with the order invoked in her essays, it is necessary to recognise the metaphysical depreciation of history; the entropy inherent in the passage of time as it is taught (though not exclusively) in the Hindu theories of the unfolding of the cosmic cycles. Each complete cycle's unfolding is divided into four Yugas, and with the passing of each Yuga a quarter of reality is removed from common apprehension until the complete cycle is exhausted—from the highest qualitative possibilities to the lowest: from the 'golden age' to the age of metaphysical poverty in which material qualities are the determining measure of all values, in which state, as Kathleen Raine often points out, 'ignorance passes judgement on knowledge'. At this point the higher, qualitative wisdom is excluded from contributing to the contextual understanding of the arts of life. As becomes evident from, for instance, her essay 'On the Symbol', in addition to its inherent presence in the 'learning of the Imagination' of the poets she studied, the guiding source of the teaching of the perennial wisdom the author draws upon she found in seminal texts of René Guénon. Speaking of the law of correspondence, as it operates throughout phenomenal and noumenal worlds, the poet quotes a key passage from Guénon's *Symbolism of the Cross*:

> By virtue of this law, each thing, proceeding as it does from a metaphysical principle from which it derives all its reality, translates or expresses that principle in its own fashion and in accordance with its own order of existence, so that from one order to another all things are linked together and correspond in such a way as to contribute to the universal and total harmony, which, in the multiplicity of manifestation, can be likened to a manifestation of the principial unity itself. For this reason the laws of a lower domain can always be taken to symbolise realities of a higher order, wherein resides their own profoundest cause, which is at once their principle and their end.

The Hindu teaching of the Yugas, as the poet pointed out in her monumental study of the sources of William Blake's iconography, *Blake and Tradition*, allows us to infer 'that the natural world may ... degenerate and withdraw its qualities and powers from degenerate civilisations like our own, following the loss of certain faculties of (qualitative) perception'. This seemingly bleak assessment is none the less, on the evidence, a realistic one, and the poet did not shy away from its wider implications in her attempt to demonstrate the deforming of the arts of our time when isolated from the perennial wisdom. In her essay 'Poetic Symbols as a Vehicle of Tradition' the poet, asking whether or not 'we are the last of the old', points out,

> There is a sense in which the relating of past to future is always the work of any present; and a single generation may at any time risk the whole continuity of civilisation and learning. Ages of accumulation are entrusted to each generation by the

past, desiring to make over its treasures to the use of the future. But we all have at this time the sense of a situation unprecedented, of the end of a cycle of that Great Year of the ancients which has again become a powerful symbol at the present time.

So we have to ask if it could be at all possible that there may yet be a late flowering from the seed of the ancient knowledge in the degenerate civilisation we have created by default, according to the prevailing decadent conditions? T.S. Eliot went so far as to suggest our civilisation might perhaps be the first to leave behind no culture.

In the same essay Kathleen Raine asserts, of the cosmic decline of the gradual movement from qualitative to quantitative possibilities, that it is not from a 'failure to be or become what they should be, but rather through their own fulfilment, when all the seeds sown at the beginning have come to fruition', and the 'governing spirit' (as Plato called it) of the universe recedes. The Platonic teaching is fully in accord with the Hindu in its metaphysical essence. Transposed to the study of European culture, the poet repeatedly traced (as she does in her essay 'On the Symbol') the line of descent of the life-giving learning of the traditional wisdom in the West, from Plato and the Neoplatonists to the Florentine renaissance to Edmund Spenser, up to Yeats and beyond, each in their way making a stand against the unfolding, temporal exhaustion. Far removed as they might seem, such desiderata lend a powerful advocacy to Kathleen Raine finding in Eliot the most eloquent spokesperson among her contemporaries of the loss of vision of the sacred that is the hallmark of what the French scholar Henry Corbin called modern man's 'agnostic reflex'. A revealing indication of the gradual erosion of the transcendent as a vital attribute is in the absence in contemporary arts of a sense of hierarchy as the embodiment of beauty informing the creative process. In 'The Use of the Beautiful' the poet writes,

> Since the beautiful is an order of wholes, and of wholeness, a mask of its informing presence is the symmetry and pattern of verse. It is impossible to speak of beauty without speaking of form. Beauty is a unity, a unification; and lyric form, as all

poets know, comes from something 'given', precisely when imaginative inspiration is strongest.

The further we go back in history the more readily we must acknowledge that the arts immemorially served as the means by which man integrates himself within the total cosmic fabric in accordance with their reciprocal spiritual nature. In the same essay the author points to this rejection of beauty in the contemporary arts as indicative of the unconscious reaction to the absence of any relation to the total cosmic reality. Beauty, the poet suggests, possesses an inherent reproach, which reproach—given the active presence of an adequate perception—harbours a proof that the essence of our human state lies beyond the limitations of mundane reality. In the sensory consolation that beauty offers, we might find some intimation of our perfection in the eternal. Perhaps it should be said, in parenthesis, that it is not so much a rejection of beauty in the modern arts, so much as that beauty simply becomes beyond the reach of art for want of its adequate perception. The consequence is clear. The all too evident 'realism' of the demotic unfailingly equates the human condition with the lowest possibilities rather than the highest. Its stock-in-trade is to reflect the least significant dimension of our common experience, founded as that is on no more than the 'fortuitous concourse of memories accumulated and lost', as Blake pertinently observed.

Time and again in her essays, Kathleen Raine, in arguing for the value of poetry as a living presence in 'the house of the soul' (the phrase is I. A. Richards's), questions whether the arts of 'self-expression' can serve any purpose beyond being a minor diversion from the business of maintaining our bodily survival. The comprehensiveness of the author's standpoint enables her to point up the terms by which the arts might enhance and enrich the human condition, but also the terms on which they debase and pervert that condition.

Despite their commitment to the perennial wisdom, which none the less includes a recognition of its by now, in the modern mind, almost complete obsolescence—at least so far as the arts are involved —the poet's essays may be read as offering the hope of retrieving some reverberation of the archetypal order in which knowledge is a vital, intuitive state of being rather than an accumulation of observed and rationalised information largely handed down, often on questionable authority and rarely verified in the direct under-standing of the knower. The essays underwrite a recognition that 'culture' is much more than the mere outcome of 'what people do'. They are a reminder that the word culture has its semantic roots in the notion of cultivation; and what is to be cultivated is, precisely, the potential spirituality of the integral human state.

The traditional hierarchy of values that comprises the perennial wisdom cannot, by its very nature, be destroyed. 'Reality', as the poet reminds us, 'is always and everywhere itself'. According to the primordial wisdom, the soul and the world are mirrored in each other. Man looks into nature to find the soul of the Creation so that the world is apprehended as a living presence, an incarnational immediacy of Being that is experienced as the world's noumenal significance. In her essay 'The Underlying Order' the poet speaks of the living source of love that makes this mutual embrace possible, in these terms:

> Plotinus wrote of 'felicity' as the goal and natural term of all
> life, and attributed it not only to man and animals but to
> plants also. Beatitude—felicity—is not an accident of being
> and consciousness: it is our very nature to seek, and to attain,
> joy; and it is for the arts to hold before us images of our eternal
> nature, through which we may awaken to, and grow towards,
> that reality which is our humanity itself.

In the poetry of each of her chosen subjects there is the implicit acknowledgement that the function of *poesis* is to guard the invio-late world of Imagination as the bond that joins transcendent and sensible orders of reality. In her commentary on these poets the author relentlessly points to the catastrophe that is the abolition of poetry's guardianship of beauty in the modern world. The crisis is stark and unequivocal: the Creator can be found only in and through the reciprocal love of the Creator and the Creation. Even more: in the final, metaphysical analysis there is only God; there is only God to witness God: 'the divine seeking the divine'. The materialism against which the poet was embattled does not present us with a 'face' of the real with which we might conduct a dialogue concerning the divinity of our personhood. All cultural meanings and values rest, finally, on such an exchange. In the modern world-view, based as it is on sensate awareness, as the poet writes in an essay on Yeats, 'the age-old search for truth and beauty and the good has been replaced by the observable, the immediate, and the process of change as values in themselves'.

⊕

Arguably the most important overarching theme of Kathleen Raine's thought is that of the nature and function of Imagination. Whether explicitly or implicitly, the poet's essays raise the broader question: What is the ontological status of an image held in the mind?

Throughout the essays the word imagination is often given a cap-ital initial. For the poet, as for her master, Blake, Imagination is the supreme faculty by which true poetic vision achieves the fulfilment of its intrinsic quality as the agent of spiritual perception. Here we are far from the commonplace idea of imagination as simply the passive mirror of images drawn from the sensorium, a view that leaves unanswered the question, in what sense can it be said that such images are 'real' or 'unreal'?

For Kathleen Raine Imagination is theophanic vision and is thereby a transcendent faculty: the capital indicates the distinction. In Imagination we are the very act of apprehending the Sacred in participative mode, in and through images that render cognitive experience as inherently meaningful. True Imagination does not invent or impose meaning. In the truly Imaginative image, the soul arrives at the necessity to inhabit experience as an act of Being, fac-ing the presence of its meaning in relation to the Supreme Reality—an act of ultimate sympathetic correspondence. This is not to sug-gest that the poet's conception of Imagination is 'illustrated' in her poems. But I would draw attention to her 'Northumbrian Sequence' as a poem that inhabits the conception outlined above.

These essays are nothing if not an impassioned argument for the recovery of the poetic image as an authentic approach to sacred reality. The author's argument starts from Blake's assertion that active Imagination presents images of 'what eternally exists, really and unchangeably'. But from that position to confronting the materialist bias of the modern mind for which imagination is merely a passively reflective faculty, and for which anything that is not quantitative substance is in some way unreal—in other words, a fiction—involves a considerable leap.

Although the concept of a spiritually active Imagination, largely learned from Blake, is present in the poet's earlier scholarly work, in the essays of her later years the poet took strength from the work of Henry Corbin. Expounding the Sufi doctrine of the *mundus imaginalis*, based mainly on the Illuminationist School of Persian mysticism (Suhrawardi, Ibn 'Arabi and Mulla Sadra), in order to recover for the West the true cognitive status of the Imagination, Corbin showed how the *mundus imaginalis* is an intermediary domain in the mystic's journey to the One 'where the spiritual takes body and the body becomes spiritual'. It provides therein the essential link that joins in total continuity the forms of the corporeal world as subsisting in the forms of the spiritual substance of the intelligible world. The *mundus imaginalis*, so understood, Corbin called the 'exultation' of the Imagination. It

> articulates three categories of universe . . . physical sensory world . . . the supersensory world of the Soul . . . the universe of pure archangelic Intelligences. To these three universes correspond three organs of knowledge: the senses, the imagination, and the intellect, a triad to which corresponds the triad of anthropology: body, soul, spirit.
>
> We observe immediately that we are no longer reduced to the dilemma of thought and extension, to the schema of a cosmology and a gnoseology limited to the empirical world and the world of abstract understanding. Between the two is placed an intermediate world . . . the world of the Image, *mundus imaginalis*: a world as ontologically real as the world of the senses and the world of the intellect, a world that requires a faculty of perception belonging to it, a faculty that is a cogni-

tive function, a *noetic* value, as fully real as the faculties of sensory perception or intellectual intuition. This faculty is the imaginative power, the one we must avoid confusing with the imagination that modern man identifies with 'fantasy' and that, according to him, produces only the 'imaginary'.[†]

There is no doubt room for a close scrutiny of the poet's appropriation of the concept of the *imaginal* world (Corbin himself invented the term *mundus imaginalis* to denote the realm in which imaginative consciousness is spiritually active) in order to counter the modern acceptance of imagination as having a merely passive function. This appropriation does give rise to certain problems, the most serious of which is the danger of divinising Imagination itself. I must leave others better qualified to examine the problems that arise in any attempt to transpose from the cadre of Islamic spirituality, a framework for understanding the spirituality of the poetic Imagination. However that may be, it should be clear why the poet made use of Corbin's studies.

In light of this it is not difficult to see what the ultimate aim of Kathleen Raine's challenge to the materialist premises as to the nature of mind was. The imaginative discourse of the poet, if it is to have an authentic spiritual status, must have a place from which to speak of the 'unseen' realities that inform the significance of the world of sensible appearances. And that discourse must possess a language whose voice is capable of embracing, and therefore speaking of, *things* beyond the transient world. In short, the language of the poet must, in some authentic fashion, identify with the ultimate source of which it speaks. This is the alchemy of metaphysical analogy. It has always been acknowledged that the voice of the poet occupies the highest eminence when it comes to articulating the intrinsic spiritual aspirations of man to inhabit his ultimate home, beyond his 'exile' on earth. It is where he locates the *meaning* of his mundane life. As the poet states in 'The Underlying Order':

[†] This passage is taken from Corbin's essay '"*Mundus Imaginalis*" or the Imaginary and the Imaginal' in *Swedenborg and Esoteric Islam* (West Chester, PA: Swedenborg Foundation, 1995), to which the reader is directed.

[W]ithin the tradition of spiritual knowledge which I have indicated, the underlying order is not some system of natural laws but being itself, at once the 'person' and 'place' of the universe. Within this whole we are, in our present state, aware only of the limited field of our own lives. We are aware of other lives, and the great fields beyond us, other times and places and being and modes of being surrounding us like unexplored forests or unclimbed mountains or unsailed seas. A sort of fragrance, or music, is sometimes borne to us on an invisible wind from those far-off fields of knowledge and experience, and we wish we could experience more of that whole of which each of us is at once an infinitesimal part and an infinite centre.

Such a passage gives every reason to recognise that the poet's essays are not intended as an academic exercise in erudition—a contribution to 'Eng. Lit.'—but are addressed to the soul of the reader.

As the poet argues in her essays and presents in her poetry, and from the position of addressing a literary convention so long confined to the ephemeralities of 'self-expression', it seems likely that the only dependable way to the restoration of the poet's true vocation is through a heightened perception that shares something of the experience of the contemplative mystic providing a template as to how the forms of the natural world are to be truly perceived. Mystical experience has in all cultures been taken to be evidence that phenomenal nature is illuminated when regarded as a shadow of the supranatural. We are back to those bright shadows on the wall of the Platonic cave. Perhaps the question to what extent the poetic symbol can ever have quite the ontological status of the *imaginal* image must remain unanswerable. Be that as it may, in her essays, devoted as they are to the 'learning of the Imagination', Kathleen Raine cogently suggest that such study can support the transmutation if guided by the predilections of the illuminated soul. In a world of impermanence it is the nature of mind to arrest the fleeting: to find confirmation beyond sensory perception, not a substitute for the real, but the Real itself; a world made evident through the poetic language of symbolic discourse. As Frithjof Schuon has pointed out, 'the symbol is a suggestion aiming at an intuition, not an explanation addressing a thought'.

The work of each of the poets to whom Kathleen Raine addressed an essay challenged the secularism of their time which, as she puts it in her comments on 'Ash Wednesday', seeks 'to obliterate from modern experience the old vision of human love as something holy, sacramental'. Seen in that light we see that the essays are not a contribution to 'literature', so much as an attempt at an enlargement of our being as a corrective to those diminishments that have ended up converting imaginative consciousness into cyber-space where there is no principle or measure of significance and where profundity and platitude are indistinguishable.

We can hardly doubt that this is largely the reason why the arts now fight to secure a modest territory from which to make a meaningful contribution to the quality of life. With each generation the gulf between the cultures that gave us, in Yeats's phrase, 'monuments of unageing intellect' and contemporary culture grows deeper and wider. At the same time, ever more sophisticated means of retrieval and storage of those past cultures is pressed into service. This making available in curatorial form the material remains of so many past cultures is paradoxically accompanied, not by a sense of guidance and illumination as to their spiritual wealth, but a pervasive sense of surfeit and exhaustion. In recognition of this it hardly seems audacious of the poet to suggest that we live in the first society to build no environment for the arts—that is to say, worthy 'monuments' of our own. The essays more than hint at the coming barbarism. Without what is *signified*, we are mere creatures of biological process. If so, by what principle of permanence do we measure the flow? Without the value of permanence, what must be the obvious function of intelligence, to evaluate, is neutralised in the face of an incomprehensible mystery. At the end of her essay on 'Vernon Watkins and the Bardic Tradition' the poet noted:

> What we did not know thirty years ago was how extreme
> would be the isolation of those who hold to tradition. It then
> seemed that there were at least some values which were agreed
> upon between the profane positivist world and the world of

the 'ancient springs'. . . . We can no longer deceive ourselves. It seems that there no longer exist any common terms or values; beyond a certain point of divergence communication becomes impossible. . . . Tradition, which recognises a difference between knowledge and ignorance, cannot come to terms with a world in which there are no longer any standards by which truth or falsehood may be measured.

We are living the ever-widening divergence.

That there could never be a return to the old order of cultural values should be perfectly obvious. It would, were it even remotely possible, amount to such a reversal of premises as would rend what, over countless generations, has been recognised to be the properly human fabric of life. The 'signs of the times' are that the unfolding cycle must exhaust *all* its possibilities, the lowest not excluded, before a new cycle can begin. Are we then to conclude that our lot is one of unabated confusion and further degeneration? Is there nothing we can do to alleviate the now almost total erosion of even the humanist culture, itself an attrition of the traditional cultures founded, ultimately, on sacred principles? Are we to be forever imprisoned by the futility of living in a world where our subjectivity is bound within a closed circuit of accounting and measuring its existential activity without recourse to its ineffaceable source? The poet offered her response to such questions in the long concluding paragraph of 'What Is Man?'

Our materialist secular society, well though it may educate in the natural sciences, altogether fails to educate the human soul, the invisible humanity which is, in Plato's words as well as Blake's, 'the true man'. We are simply not educated in these things which above all make us human. Those who inherit—who have not yet lost, under the cancerous impact of Western ideologies—some metaphysical, religious and iconographic tradition, some language of symbolic images built up through-out a civilisation, are fortunate indeed. For the rest of us, all is to be remade; not altogether as if it had never been, for in the relics, the survivals of the past, we can rediscover lost knowledge, piece by piece reconstructing something, perhaps, which will serve a broken culture without a tradition of its own. Reality is always and everywhere itself; but who shall say whether we can use the language of Christendom, of the Far East, of Islam (the last prophetic revelation), of Jungian psychology, of Cabbala, of the American Indians? In all the arts there is a confusion of tongues. Blake knew everything except how to find symbolic or linguistic terms to communicate what he knew; he was eclectic in his symbols but orthodox in his Christian theology. Yeats's lifelong labour was to test, to discard or to retain, a great range of symbols and terms drawn from many traditions, Rosicrucian, neo-Platonic, Far Eastern. To recreate a common language for the communication of knowledge of spiritual realities, and of the invisible order of the psyche, is the problem now for any serious artist or poet, as it should be for educators. Yet the problem of language would resolve itself once these worlds were re-opened to our experience for the knowledge itself is primary, the terms—symbols—secondary. This rediscovery, re-learning, is a long hard task—a lifelong task for those who undertake it; yet the most rewarding of all tasks, since it is a work of self-discovery which is at the same time a universal knowledge, 'knowledge absolute' as the Vedas claim. So-called 'creativity' and 'self-expression' will not get us very far. The Grecian goldsmith, the Gothic sculptor, the painter of churches or elaborator of Islamic geometric patterns in a mosque were none of them 'expressing themselves' in the modern sense of the term; far less breaking with the past, or being 'revolutionary'. They were making use of the shared knowledge of a spiritual tradition that illuminates their work, as it illuminated the inner lives of those who participated in its unity of culture.

For all our failings we remain human, and on that evidence it is worthy to believe that to recognise an 'end' is already to acknowledge a criterion that transcends whatever powers carry us to the end and is not itself a component of the final collapse, being that by which the end is measured; where we then must ask, 'What next?'

We end with a passage from 'The Vertical Dimension':

We are told that 'In the beginning was the Word, and the Word was with God and the Word was God.' That is an amazing claim to make for language, for it points to a source that used to be called 'inspiration' when people spoke of such things— the 'inspired' Word of God, a God (if one dare use the word) who 'spake by the prophets', and what else is the spirit of prophecy (Blake asks) but 'the poetic genius'? If the name of poet is still held in honour is it not because it still carries with it a certain remote echo of that age-old belief that the poet is 'inspired'? An honour due to poetry only when, and insofar as, it does, in a measure, aspire to participation in a sacred vision of the Word that is 'with God', on that vertical ladder which has in our time for the most part been lost?

Afterword

The Making of a Canon: A Memoir

ALTHOUGH THE GOLGONOOZA EDITION of *The Collected Poems of Kathleen Raine* was published in 2000, its origins went back some fifteen years before that. By the late 1980s it became evident that stocks of the Allen & Unwin *Collected Poems* of 1981 were running low and that, when it finally sold out, there would be nothing of Kathleen's poetry in print. I had already been working with her on a new volume of poems, which became *The Presence* of 1987. During this period I had several times suggested that, seeing there had never been such, a *Selected Poems* would be a good idea. To my surprise the poet was reluctant to show any interest in such a project. Indeed, she gave me the impression that her past work was of little concern to her, although she obviously made something of an exception to this lack of interest with her poetry readings.

I think I must have said to her at some point during the work on *The Presence* that if she allowed her past poetry to completely disappear so far as being in print was concerned, there was a good chance it would be lost for at least a generation. I think I had heard it said that if a poet's work is unavailable at the time of their death this has been found to be the case. After proposing the idea several times I finally got her to agree to the project, and she undertook the task, with some input from me, with not exactly a great deal of enthusiasm, as I recall. In the event the volume, published in 1988, was a considerable success, selling well for many years and eventually being reprinted twice: six thousand copies in all!

In 1992 a further volume of new poems, *Living with Mystery*, was published, its content, as with *The Presence*, being selected from the larger body of work written at that period. By the year 1999 there were more new poems, though not enough, as we judged, for a new volume. In the year or so approaching her ninetieth birthday it slowly became evident, to me at least, that a radical review of her poetic legacy was called for.

Selected Poems was by now looking like a very unrepresentative gathering of her poetry over all, in view of the fact that it contained nothing from what must be seen as her major poetic achievement, *On a Deserted Shore* of 1973, and there had since been two new collections as well as a growing body of poems yet to be collected.

On several occasions I suggested a new *Collected Poems*, an idea that was always met with a most emphatically negative response: 'You can do all that when I'm dead' was the inevitable reply. The poet was not to be moved on this matter.

Although I did not recognise the deeper reason for this negativity at the time, I certainly did notice the stern, cold look of self-reproval that came over her face whenever the subject was mooted. I had seen that look several times over the years; at its most chilling (for me) at a party at her house in Paulton's Square at a time when Wendell Berry was visiting England, to attend, I think, one of the two Temenos Conferences held at Dartington. Most of Kathleen's then living illustrious friends were present at what was, for all but her, it seemed, a most hospitable and congenial occasion. In the midst of much pleasure at sharing good company and eager conversation among friends who, for the most part, would have had little opportunity to assemble in this way, I caught sight of Kathleen sitting utterly and coldly stony-faced, seemingly totally unaware of the surrounding congeniality. It was as if, unseen by everyone else, the messenger of Rilke's 'Alcestis' had come among us to summon her.

I realised that I needed some way of overcoming her implacable resistance to the idea of a *Collected Poems* in her lifetime. For two or three years, I could find no solution. Eventually, one evolved over several weeks took shape as I came to realise that the archival spirit of our age, posthumously let loose upon her poetic oeuvre, would determine an outcome that she could never approve. It had already happened, with ungainly results, to a number of her deceased contemporaries. There began the fashion for the 'Complete Poems' in which what one had been accustomed to accept as a 'Collected' was suddenly stretched to an extent, sometimes two, sometimes three times the size. This trend to including everything that could be salvaged of a poet's work ran far beyond what might be regarded as the decent necessity of a 'Collected' that included only the work a poet might regard as worthy of perpetuation in print. In this I saw my chance.

I marshalled my argument and carefully put it to the poet. I pointed out that, due to her age she was, so far as I knew, uniquely placed of any previous English poet of stature, to look back on six decades of her work and to decide what exactly she wanted her poetic canon to be. In brief, what, of all her poetry, she would want posthumously to be judged by.

It was well known that, in the past, the poet had, somewhat ruthlessly, some had thought, suppressed much of her early poetry. With this precedent in mind, I was sure she would not want everything she had written to form her poetic legacy. I pointed out that if she did not take this opportunity to determine the extent and value of her canon, then eventually someone (not Golgonooza, the end of whose active life was already in sight) would collect every scrap that could be found to comprise a 'Complete Poems'. 'God, I don't want that', was her now revised and equally emphatic response. So it was we set about the work necessary to make the *Collected Poems* of her choosing.

It was agreed that we would assemble everything that could be found: published volumes, printed poems (in journals and magazines), and a very miscellaneous collection of typescripts, sometimes of determinate, sometimes indeterminate age. These would have included material from Golgonooza's accumulating archive as well as the poems rejected from *The Presence* and *Living with Mystery* and, of course, the new poems written after the publication of the latter volume.

Once amassed, three sets of this large collection were made: one copy for the author, another for me, with a third set going to Grevel Lindop. We were to mark each poem with either a tick, a cross or a question mark. So far as I recall, we were, as was perhaps to be expected, in broad agreement about ticks and crosses, differing mostly on question marks. Grevel returned his copy to me, I collated his marks with my own set and then, over several meetings, Kathleen and I worked over the sets until we came to an agreement about inclusions. There was little contention in these discussions, each of several hours, and on only a few occasions did we find it difficult to agree; especially when it began to look as if the final contents would make what we both felt would be too large a volume. Kathleen was anxious to keep the final choice within certain bounds: 'After all, Brian, even justly famous poets are mostly remembered for a handful of their poems', I recall her saying during our discussions.

There were no manuscripts of material written before the 1970s (so far as we could determine), and nothing she had rejected from her earlier volumes when compiling the *Collected Poems* of 1981 was reinstated.

One curiosity emerged after her death. When I was going over the papers left in her writing desk I found a wallet folder at the top of the papers in the top right-hand drawer (as if deliberately placed there so as to come readily to notice), a part collection of poems written, I think, in the 1960s. Apparently, as I later had confirmed by her daughter Anna and friend of longstanding, Thetis Blacker, during a period in which the poet feared she had 'dried up', she settled into the habit each morning of opening the Bible at random, placing a finger on the page and then writing spontaneously a 'poem' on whatever was forthcoming as a result. From the numbering on the part of the typescript that had survived in the wallet folder, it was evident that there were in excess of one hundred of these 'poems'. These were read, at intervals, to Anna and Thetis who were in agreement that the results were not a success. I can confirm that their judgement was sound on the evidence of what the folder contained. Kathleen, we must suppose, decided they were not worthy candidates for consideration when it came to amassing work to be judged fit for the canon. Certainly these 'poems' were never offered at the time of our deliberations. But why, after all those years, were they placed so conspicuously in the desk drawer?

There was one poem about which we could not agree: 'The Messengers', from the poet's first volume, *Stone and Flower*. Kathleen wanted to leave it out but for some reason I was at a loss to justify why I was reluctant to reject it. We went over and over it without reaching agreement, still determined to settle the matter to my satisfaction. Quite suddenly I saw that the poem effectively ended at the penultimate stanza and that the last three lines somehow dissolved unsatisfactorily the tension of the poem into something too explanatory, too self-consciously rounded off. 'Brilliant!' the poet exclaimed. The cut was made. After publication one reader wrote in to point out that the last stanza had been mistakenly left out. Not so.

Now I am not so sure. If it were possible to relive the opportunity, I would let the cross prevail in favour of another poem that first appeared in *Living in Time*, albeit without its penultimate 'with'. It was subsequently included, with correction, in the first *Collected* of 1956 but dropped for the second, where *Living in Time* was severely pruned. It is a much stronger poem than 'The Messengers', with form and content more convincingly integrated. I cannot now imagine how we let this one slip through the net, and must assume the author had very personal reasons, connected with Gavin Maxwell, for rejecting it.

Winged Eros

A thought new-born rises from my delight
With bird-like eyes and wings
Turning in air to angel and to rose.

Bird that can cross the distance of interior skies,
Fly to where my love beside the blue sea lies,
Wake in his dream while to the world he sleeps.

Angel, be of my soul the gold messenger
To fill his heart unspeakably with prayer,
And in a wind pass through his house like fire.

Rose dye his veins in crimson of your blood,
Rose at his heart your mystery unfold
And with your sharp thorns wound him with desire.

I would also have argued to alter, in the last line, the first 'with' to 'let'.

From getting Kathleen to agree to undertake the project to the day of publication took eighteen months.

To return to the question of the poet's earlier opposition to reviewing her earlier work. I should say that she showed no lack of enthusiasm about poems written in the years I knew her—1968 to her death in 2003. She was very keen that *The Presence* should appear and later *Living with Mystery*.

Here I must enter to some extent into the realms of speculation. I would not want to go so far as to claim certainty in every detail of what follows concerning the causes of her opposition. But you cannot have a close relationship with someone for over thirty years without coming to some understanding of what motivates them, what disturbs them and what pains them.

I have no doubt that, as a result of the great many intimate meetings we had over the years, and especially over the eighteen months we worked on this project, for the poet the task was a painful one. It meant revisiting much of her past life that I suspect she had hitherto all but repressed. Although she never talked to me in any detail about her earlier life, of the years before we met (in thirty-six years she never once mentioned the name of Gavin Maxwell), I none the less discerned that they lived on in her as burdensome luggage. Many of her misgivings in this respect are, of course, the substance of her volumes of autobiography. In going over her earlier poetry the poet was no doubt obliged to relive again something of the reality of what it had cost her to write it. On three occasions, each face to face over the lunch table, in mid-editorial meeting, she said to me, with a look of chilling resignation, 'It has not been worth it'. All argument on my part to the effect that she had, in reality, no choice, whatever the cost, but to follow her vocation—she had not chosen poetry, poetry had chosen her—was to no avail. When I mentioned this to Thetis after Kathleen's death, she dismissed it as a typical piece of Kathleen's histrionics; not to be taken seriously. But there was no doubt in my mind that, whatever affectation Kathleen might have displayed to her friends in past years, this time she meant it. To me it was evident, on the basis of the many, many hours we had spent in conversation, that her vocation as a poet had at times caused much pain to many closest to her. No doubt the extent and depth of this suffering will never be disclosed to others. But for Kathleen it was an abiding reality that could not be excluded from the balance of factors one must weigh in deciding for one's self the value of a life's work.

It is, I think, worth noting that the poet's most recurrent reason for rejecting many of her earlier poems was on the grounds of their expressing personal emotion. By contrast, in her later published work, we find a more frequent inclusion of, and a greater degree of equanimity in, poems that express affiliations of emotion and friendship.

From within a culture such as ours, always freighted with the bugbear of the psychology of personality, there will always be those artists for whom the driving imperative of their art, especially in their earlier years, will in retrospect come to seem too heavy a price to have paid for that art's achievement. We have no choice but to be alert to the presiding paradox that what was for one generation a casting of shadows might become for a subsequent one a source of at least partial illumination.

Kathleen's self-judgement died with her. We are left with a body of work whose value to us it is ours to decide.

Select Bibliography

POETRY

Stone and Flower: Poems 1935–43. Drawings by Barbara Hepworth. Editions Poetry London. London: Nicholson & Watson, 1943.

Living in Time. London: Editions Poetry London, 1946.

The Pythoness and Other Poems. London: Hamish Hamilton, 1949; New York: Farrar, Straus & Young, 1952.

The Year One. London: Hamish Hamilton, 1952; New York: Farrar, Straus & Young, 1953.

The Hollow Hill and Other Poems, 1960–1964. London: Hamish Hamilton, 1965.

The Lost Country. Dublin: Dolmen Press; London: Hamish Hamilton, 1971.

On a Deserted Shore. Frontispiece by Gavin Maxwell. Dublin: Dolmen Press; London: Hamish Hamilton, 1973.

The Oval Portrait and Other Poems. London: Enitharmon Press; Hamish Hamilton, 1977.

The Oracle in the Heart and Other Poems, 1975–1978. Dublin: Dolmen Press; London: Allen & Unwin, 1980.

Collected Poems, 1935–1980. London: Allen & Unwin, 1981.

The Presence: Poems 1984–87. Ipswich: Golgonooza Press, 1987.

Selected Poems. Poems 1943–1987. Ipswich: Golgonooza Press, 1988; reprinted 1993 and 2002.

Living with Mystery: Poems 1987–91. Ipswich: Golgonooza Press, 1992; reprinted 1993.

The Collected Poems of Kathleen Raine. Ipswich: Golgonooza Press, 2000; reprinted 2008; Washington, DC: Counterpoint, 2001. Reissued as *Collected Poems*. London: Faber, 2019.

PROSE

The Story of Three Water Drops. Illustrated by Francis Rose. Fiction for children. London: Nicholson & Watson, 1946.

William Blake. Writers and Their Work, no. 12. London: Longmans, reprinted 1958; revised ed. 1965, 2nd revised ed., 1969.

Coleridge. Writers and Their Work, no. 43. London: Longmans, Green, for the British Council & National Book League, 1953; revised 1958; Longmans, 1963; reprinted with additions to bibliography, 1971.

Defending Ancient Springs. London: Oxford University Press, 1967; reprinted Ipswich: Golgonooza Press, 1985.

Blake and Tradition. 2 vols. Andrew Mellon Lectures in the Fine Arts, no. 11, Washington, DC, 1962. Bollingen series. Princeton, NJ: Princeton University Press, 1968; 1969; London: Routledge & Kegan Paul, 1969; reprinted 2002.

William Blake. World of Art Library. London: Thames & Hudson, 1970; New York: Praeger, 1971.

Faces of Day and Night. Autobiographical. London: Enitharmon Press, 1972.

Farewell Happy Fields: Memories of Childhood. London: Hamish Hamilton, 1973; New York: George Braziller, 1977.

The Land Unknown: Further Chapters of Autobiography. London: Hamish Hamilton; New York: George Braziller, 1975.

The Lion's Mouth: Concluding Chapters of Autobiography. London: Hamish Hamilton, 1977; New York: George Braziller, 1978.

Blake and Antiquity. Single-volume abridged version of *Blake and Tradition,* 1968–1969. Princeton, NJ: Princeton University Press, 1977; London: Routledge, 1979.

Blake and the New Age. Boston and London: Allen & Unwin, 1979.

The Human Face of God: William Blake and the Book of Job. London: Thames & Hudson, 1982.

The Inner Journey of the Poet and Other Papers. Edited by Brian Keeble. London: George Allen & Unwin, 1982; New York: George Braziller, 1982.

Yeats the Initiate: Essays on Certain Themes in the Writings of W. B. Yeats. Dublin: Dolmen Press; London: George Allen & Unwin, 1986.

India Seen Afar. A fourth volume of autobiography. Bideford, Devon: Green Books, 1990.

Golgonooza, City of Imagination. Last Studies in William Blake. Ipswich: Golgonooza Press, 1991.

Select Bibliography

Autobiographies. Comprising the three volumes first published 1973, 1975, 1977. London: Skoob Books, 1991.

W.B. Yeats and the Learning of the Imagination. Ipswich: Golgonooza Press, 1999.

The Underlying Order and Other Essays. Edited with an introduction by Brian Keeble. London: Temenos Academy, 2008.

That Wondrous Pattern: Essays on Poetry and Poets. Edited with an introduction by Brian Keeble. Berkeley: Counterpoint Press, 2017.

About the Author

Brian Keeble is the author of *Daily Bread: Art and Work in the Reign of Quantity* (2015); *God and Work* (2009); *Art: For Whom and for What?* (1998), and other essay collections as well as several collections of poetry, most recently *Mask after Mask* (2017). He has edited three volumes of Kathleen Raine's essays—*The Inner Journey of the Poet and Other Papers* (1982), *The Underlying Order and Other Essays* (2008), and *That Wondrous Pattern: Essays on Poetry and Poets* (2017)—and also edited her *Collected Poems* (2000). As the editor, designer, and publisher of Golgonooza Press in Ipswich, England, from 1974 to 2004, he published numerous volumes of writings related to the arts and the perennial philosophy, by authors such as Wendell Berry, Eric Gill, Seyyed Hossein Nasr, and Philip Sherrard. Keeble was one of the founders of the journal *Temenos* (London, 1980–1991), and is a fellow and former Council and Academic Board member of the Temenos Academy.

www.ingramcontent.com/pod-product-compliance
Lightning Source LLC
Chambersburg PA
CBHW021506090426

42739CB00007B/491